WRITERS AND THEIR WORK

Isobel Armstrong
Consultant Editor

T0313601

POETS
OF THE
SECOND WORLD WAR

POETS
OF THE
SECOND WORLD WAR
Douglas, Lewis, Jarrell, Causley, Simpson & Others

Rory Waterman

© 2015 by Rory Waterman

First published in 2015 by Northcote House Publishers Ltd, Mary Tavy, Tavistock, Devon, PL19 9PY, United Kingdom.
Tel: +44 (0) 1822 810066 Fax: +44 (0) 1822 810034.

British Library Cataloguing-in-Publication Data
A catalogue record for this book is available from the British Library

ISBN 978-0-7463-1279-7 hardcover
ISBN 978-0-7463-1280-3 paperback

Typeset by PDQ Typesetting, Newcastle-under-Lyme
Printed and bound by CPI Group (UK) Ltd, Croydon, CR0 4YY

Contents

Acknowledgements

Thanks and acknowledgments are due to the British Library, Martin Stannard, Michael Hanke, Libby Peake, the Estate of Charles Causley, and the Charles Causley Archives at the University of Exeter and SUNY Buffalo. A small part of this book draws on my essay 'Charles Causley and the Sea', published in *Through the Granite Kingdom: Essays on Charles Causley*, ed. Michael Hanke (Verlag Trier, 2012), as does a section of my book *Belonging and Estrangement in the Poetry of Philip Larkin, R. S. Thomas and Charles Causley* (Ashgate, 2014). Finally, I am grateful to Brian Hulme and Marian Boddy of Northcote House for patiently seeing this book into print.

Biographical Outlines

KEITH DOUGLAS (1920–1944)

1920	24 January: Keith Castellian Douglas born in Tunbridge Wells. Spends his first few years in Cranleigh, Surrey.
1926–31	Boards at Edgeborough School, Guildford.
1928	Douglas's father, also Keith, leaves. The two never meet again.
1931–8	Attends Christ's Hospital School, Horsham, Surrey.
1938	First poems published in *New Verse*.
1938–40	Attends Merton College, University of Oxford. His tutor is Edmund Blunden. In 1940 he edits university magazine *The Cherwell*.
1939	September: War is declared and Douglas enlists immediately, but his enlistment is deferred.
1940	July: Becomes a cavalry trooper in the British Army. Leaves a typescript of poems with Blunden.
1941	Poems praised by T. S. Eliot at Faber, who nevertheless does not offer publication.
	February: commissioned into Second Derbyshire Yeomanry, in Ripon.
	June: Sails for the Middle East, arriving in Egypt in August.
	October–November: joins the Sherwood Rangers Yeomanry, a cavalry unit, in Palestine, and visits Syria.
1942	February: is made a camouflage staff officer. It is a fairly safe position, and one he does not want.
	October: poems published in *Poetry London*. Battle of El Alamein begins on 23 October and four days later Douglas defies orders by driving from HQ to

	report for duty. On 28 October he is in battle.
1943	January–April: in hospital in Palestine, then on leave in Tel Aviv and Alexandria. Writes the first of his war poems.
	November: returns to England to train for the coming European campaign.
1944	Receives contracts for his war memoir (*Alamein to Zem Zem*) and a book of poems, which he wishes to publish under the title *Bête Noire*.
	6 June: commands a tank troop in the Normandy landings.
	9 June: killed in action near St Pierre.
1946	*Alamein to Zem Zem* published posthumously, with an appendix of poems, by Editions Poetry London.
1951	*Bête Noire* never materializes, but Editions Poetry London publish *Collected Poems*, ed. John Waller and G. S. Fraser.
1966	Faber publish *Collected Poems*, ed. John Waller, G. S. Fraser and J. C. Hall.

ALUN LEWIS (1915–1944)

1915	1 July: born at 16 Llanwynno Road, Cwmaman, near Aberdare in south Wales, the first of what would be four siblings. His parents are both schoolteachers.
1918	Lewis's father, Tom, injured in the Great War and discharged from active service.
1926	Is awarded a scholarship to Cowbridge Grammar School, a boarding school. Homesick much of the time, Lewis nonetheless receives great encouragement from an English teacher, Eric Reid. Starts writing short fiction and develops pacifist and anti-imperialist ideals.
1932–5	Reads History at the University College of Wales, Aberystwyth, for which he is awarded First Class Honours. Publishes short stories and a poem in *The Dragon*, the college magazine, and takes a keen interest in sports, including hockey.
1935	Awarded a postgraduate studentship at the Uni-

versity of Manchester. Dislikes the city and suffers from depression; but also publishes poems in the University magazine, *The Serpent*, and completes a thesis on the medieval Papal Legate, Ottobono.

1937   After two months in France, begins a teacher training course back in Aberystwyth.

1938   Publishes poems in *The Observer* and *Time and Tide*. Fails to find a teaching post.

September: writes articles for *The Aberdare Leader*, including one called 'If War Comes – Will I Fight?'

November: takes a temporary teaching post at Lewis Boys' School, Pengam. His position is made permanent a year later.

1939   Meets Gweno Ellis, a teacher at the nearby Mountain Ash Grammar School.

1940   May to October: enlists, and joins the Royal Engineers. Sent to Longmoor, Hants, and starts to write some of his finest poems, among them 'Raider's Dawn' and 'The Soldier'. Discovers Edward Thomas and visits his house at nearby Steep.

1941   July: marries Gweno in Gloucester, during leave, and is then posted to the Officer Cadet Training Unit in Lancashire.

His first collection of poems, *Raiders' Dawn*, is accepted for publication by Allen and Unwin.

November: begins a long correspondence with Robert Graves. Joins the Sixth Battalion of the South Wales Borderers at Woodbridge, Suffolk.

1942   March: *Raiders' Dawn* published.

Sent to the battle school at Aldeburgh, Suffolk.

October to November: Borderers are posted to India; sets sail from Liverpool aboard the *Athlone Castle*, and travels via Bahia in Brazin, and Durban in South Africa, on the way to Bombay. Journeys on to Nira, south of Poona.

1943   March: Battalion travels to Lake Kharakvasla to train for an offensive in Burma against the Japanese army.

July: takes leave in the Nilgiri Hills, where he meets and falls in love with Freda Ackroyd.

1944	January: writes his last poem, 'The Jungle'.
	February: the Borderers travel to north Burma and take up a position behind the front line, at Bawli.
	5 March: early in the morning, found dead by the officers' latrines, his revolver in his hand. Later in the month an army court of enquiry decides that the shooting was accidental.
1945	Lewis's second collection, *Ha! Ha! Among the Trumpets*, is published.

CHARLES CAUSLEY (1917–2003)

1917	24 August: Charles Stanley Causley born in Launceston, Cornwall. He would live in the town for almost all of his life. He is an only child.
1918	Charles's father, Stanley, invalided out of the Great War with a disability pension.
1924	Stanley Causley dies of pulmonary tuberculosis, probably related to his war service. Mother and son live on the brink of poverty.
1933	Leaves school and begins working as a builder's clerk.
1936–8	Publishes four one-act plays.
1940–6	Serves in the Royal Navy as a low-ranking coder during the Second World War, on board HMS *Glory*. Begins to focus on writing poems rather than fiction or plays, on the grounds that it is possible to compose and memorize poems while engaged in other occupations, but less feasible to compose plays or works of fiction.
1946	Begins teacher training at Peterborough Training College.
1948	Starts work at the National School in Launceston, the primary school he had attended as a pupil.
1951	First book of poems, *Farewell, Aggie Weston*, published by Hand and Flower Press. Many of the poems are about his experiences in the navy. A volume of short stories, *Hands to Dance*, is also published.
1953	Second book of poems, *Survivor's Leave*, published

	by Hand and Flower Press. This also contains many poems reflecting on life at war.
1957	*Union Street* published by Rupert Hart-Davis, a much bigger firm, with an introduction by Edith Sitwell. This book includes most of the poems from the two earlier collections alongside newer work, and firmly establishes Causley's reputation.
1958	Made a Fellow of the Royal Society of Literature.
1967	Awarded the Queen's Gold Medal for Poetry.
1970	Book of poems for children, *Figgie Hobbin*, published.
1971	Causley's mother dies. Charles moves out of the house they had shared to Cyprus Well, another modest house in the town.
1975	First *Collected Poems* published.
1976	Takes early retirement. Starts to travel widely, making extended visits to Australia, Germany, Canada and elsewhere in the following years.
1986	Awarded the CBE for services to poetry.
1987	*Causley at 70*, a Festschrift, is published, and includes poems and prose tributes from Philip Larkin, Ted Hughes, Roger McGough, Seamus Heaney and many others.
1992	A new *Collected Poems* is published. Further revised editions appear in 1997 and 2000.
1996	*Collected Poems for Children* published.
2003	Dies and is buried in the graveyard of St Thomas's Church, Launceston, next to his mother, and less than a hundred yards from where he had been born.

RANDALL JARRELL (1914–1965)

1914	6 May: born in Nashville, Tennessee, to Anna and Owen Jarrell.
1915	Randall's brother Charles is born. The Jarrells move to California, where Owen's family are from, and settle the following year in Long Beach.
1924	Randall's mother leaves his father and returns with the children to her native Tennessee.

1926–7	Returns to California to live with his paternal grandparents and his great grandmother. He is very happy there, but returns to his mother in the autumn of 1927.
1935	Receives his BA from Vanderbilt University, Nashville. His tutors include Robert Penn Warren, who would go on to publish Jarrell's criticism; Allen Tate, who would publish his poetry; and John Crowe Ransom. He also captains the university tennis team.
1937	Completes the coursework for his MA in English, also at Vanderbilt, and decides to write his MA thesis on A. E. Housman (completed in 1939).
1937	Ransom moves to Kenyon College in Gambier, Ohio, and Jarrell goes with him, teaching undergraduate classes for two years. He lodges with Ransom; Ransom's other lodger is Robert Lowell and the two become close friends.
1939	Takes a teaching post at the University of Texas, Austin.
1940	Marries Mackie Langham, a colleague.
1942	First collection of poems, *Blood for a Stranger*, published by Harcourt, Brace. Is more widely known as a witty, perceptive poetry critic, writing for *New Republic*, *The Nation* and other publications.
1943	Joins the US army in February. Is eventually assigned to the Davis-Monthon base in Arizona. He trains to become a pilot but fails aptitude tests for motion sickness and instead becomes a celestial navigation tower operator.
1945	*Little Friend, Little Friend* is published. This contains many of Jarrell's war poems.
1946–7	Becomes temporary literary editor for the *The Nation*, and lives in New York.
1947	Takes an academic post at the Woman's College of North Carolina, Greensboro.
1948	*Losses* published. This is Jarrell's second and final book of poems to concentrate on the experiences of war.
1951	Meets a mature student, Mary von Schrader, at a conference in Colorado. The two fall in love and

	Jarrell and Mackie divorce. Schrader marries Jarrell the following year. *The Seven League Crutches*, his fourth book of poems, published.
1953	First prose book, *Poetry and the Age*, published.
1956	Becomes the consultant in poetry at the Library of Congress (now known as the US Poet Laureate) and serves for two years, before returning to Greenboro.
1960	*The Woman at the Washington Zoo: Poems and Translations* published.
1963–5	Becomes mentally unwell towards the end of 1963. Is prescribed Elavil, a newly available mood-elevating drug, and his behaviour becomes increasingly erratic. In early 1965 he is taken off Elavil, becomes depressed, and ends up back in hospital having slashed his wrist.
1965	*The Lost World*, his final collection of poems, is published.
1965	11 October: hit by a car and killed. Injuries deemed consistent with accidental death.

LOUIS SIMPSON (1923–2012)

1923	27 March: Louis Aston Marantz Simpson born in Kingston, Jamaica, to Aston and Rosalind Simpson. His father is of Scottish and African ancestry; his mother is born in Russia, and has Jewish heritage: she had moved to Jamaica to act in silent movies.
1930s	Attends an English-style boarding school in Jamaica.
1939	His parents divorce and then his father dies.
1940	Louis emigrates to the USA, and attends Columbia University in New York.
1943	Joins the army. Is briefly in the tank corps, then in the 101st Airborne Division, a light infantry division trained for air assault operations. Becomes a runner, responsible for passing orders between the company headquarters and officers on the front line.
1944	6 June onwards: takes part in Operation Overlord (the D-Day landings in Normandy), and is there-

	after involved in the liberation of France, Belgium and the Netherlands. Awarded US military honours: two Purple Hearts (for being wounded on active service) and a Bronze Star (for meritorious acts in a combat zone).
1945	Suffers post-traumatic stress syndrome and spends six months in a psychiatric hospital.
1948	Receives his bachelor's degree.
1949	Travels to France with an education grant offered to returning soldiers, and studies at the University of Paris.
1949	First poetry collection, *The Arrivistes: Poems 1940–1949*, published whilst Simpson is in Paris. Marries Jeanne Rogers.
1950	Receives his masters' degree from Columbia and begins working at Bobbs-Merrill, a New York publishing house.
1954	Divorces Jeanne, with whom he has one son.
1955	Second poetry collection, *Good News of Death*, published.
1955	Marries Dorothy Roochvarg.
1955	Becomes an instructor at Columbia whilst undertaking a PhD.
1959	Third poetry collection, *A Dream of Governors: Poems*, published.
1959	Awarded his doctorate, and takes a post at the University of California, Berkeley.
1964	Wins the Pulitzer Prize for Poetry for *At the End of the Open Road* (1963). This book is typically acerbic in its analysis of modern American life, but moves away from the ballads and blank verse that had distinguished his style thus far, in favour of a more organic free verse.
1965	*Selected Poems* published.
1967	Returns to New York, and takes a post at the State University of New York, Stony Brook.
1975	*Three on the Tower*, a critical book focusing on T. S. Eliot, Ezra Pound and William Carlos Williams, published.
1979	Divorces Dorothy, with whom he has one son and one daughter.

1983	*People Live Here: Selected Poems 1949–83* published.
1985	Marries Miriam Bachner.
1989	*Selected Prose* published.
1993	Takes retirement from his job at SUNY, Stony Brook.
1997	*Modern Poets of France: A Bilingual Anthology* (1997) published, and wins the Harold Morton Landon Translation Award.
1998	Divorces Miriam.
2003	*The Owner of the House: New Collected Poems* published.
2009	*Struggling Times* published. It will be his last collection of new poems.
2010	*Voices in the Distance: Selected Poems* published.
2012	14 September: dies at home in Stony Brook, New York, of complications from Alzheimer's.

Abbreviations

CP	Randall Jarrell, *The Complete Poems* (Noonday, 1969)
CCP	Charles Causley, *Collected Poems: 1951–2000* (Picador, 2000)
CPAL	Alun Lewis, *Collected Poems of Alun Lewis*, ed. Cary Archard (Seren, 1994)
FQ	T. S. Eliot, *Four Quartets* (Faber, 1959)
LRJ	Randall Jarrell, *The Letters of Randall Jarrell*, ed. Mary Jarrell (Houghton Mifflin, 1985)
OH	Louis Simpson, *The Owner of the House: New Collected Poems 1940–2001* (BOA Editions, 2003)
PM	Keith Douglas, *A Prose Miscellany*, ed. Desmond Graham (Carcanet, 1985)
PSWW	*Poetry of the Second World War: An International Anthology*, ed. Desmond Graham (Pimlico, 1998)
TCP	Keith Douglas, *The Complete Poems*, ed. Desmond Graham, 3rd edn. (Faber, 1998)

1

Introduction:
Where Were the War Poets?

It is received wisdom that the First World War – or Great War – was also the greatest of all wars in terms of the poetry it generated, and that the Second World War inspired very little poetry to rival it. Certainly, the First World War was the subject of an extraordinary amount of worthwhile and sometimes deeply moving contemporaneous poetry – indeed, it was the first war in which the term 'war poet' had been widely applied (and applicable) to English-language writers. As this book attempts to demonstrate, though, the claim is something of an over-simplification.

Nonetheless, partially because the poetry took people by surprise during the First World War whereas they had grown to expect it in the Second, the belief was perpetuated almost from the beginning. In 1941, Robert Graves, a prominent poet associated with the Great War, gave a talk on British radio entitled 'Why has this War produced no War Poets?' and it was a question many in Britain were asking.[1] Two years later, Keith Douglas, now ironically the most celebrated of all poets associated with the Second World War, wrote an essay called 'Poets of this War' in which he asked why there were 'no poets like Owen and Sassoon who lived with the fighting troops and wrote of their experiences while they were enduring them'. He concluded that though the war might ultimately have its own poetry, it would most likely be 'created after war is over' (*PM* 119–20).

Between 1939 and 1945, relatively few active servicemen were publishing strong poetry about their experiences. Why should this have been so? To answer that question, it is first of all

1

important to consider the fundamental differences in feeling between the conscripts and enlistees of both wars. In October 1914, three months after the outbreak of the First World War and when many believed the fighting would be over by Christmas, Rupert Brooke spoke for many British soldiers with his sonnet 'Peace'. It started by thanking God for having 'matched us with His hour', and compared being sent to fight to an act of cleansing and release, 'as swimmers into cleanness leaping'.[2] Brooke died the following April and never saw active service; those who did became bogged down in a horrifying and apparently futile stalemate that went on far longer than anyone could have imagined. The British conscripts of 1939 therefore had a fairly diabolical notion of what their duty might entail. The horror of technologized war was not in itself a shock – though in fact most of the Second World War was not fought in trenches but on the move. There was little need to tell the population back home about the awfulness of warfare. In addition, there was evidently a feeling among some poets in the Second World War that pretty much everything that could be said about carnage already had been. In 'Desert Flowers', Douglas notes, as an aside and not entirely truthfully, 'Rosenberg I only repeat what you were saying' (*TCP* 108).[3]

Moreover, the Second World War had an obvious enemy. The need to defeat Fascism provided a far more identifiable central objective, however controversial many of the tactics might have been. As Michael Foss puts it in his introduction to the anthology *Poetry of the World Wars*, the latter conflict 'had a kind of moral necessity that was not apparent in the earlier blind folly'.[4] In 1943 Cecil Day Lewis, who spent the war with the Ministry of Information, published a short poem called 'Where Are the War Poets?', which implicitly accepted the validity of its titular question and provided an answer:

> It is the logic of our times,
> No subject for immortal verse –
> That we who lived by honest dreams
> Defend the bad against the worse.[5]

The war is too much the result of 'logic' to be a 'subject for immortal verse'. Day Lewis's is anything but a patriotic poem, claiming as it does that the fighting amounts to 'Defend[ing] the bad against the worse', but nonetheless it certainly makes clear that there is something – land, but perhaps also humanity – to be defended. There might have been little enthusiasm for the war, little to fight *for*, but there was plenty to fight *against*. Most poets on the allied side, and hence most Anglophone poets, viewed war against Nazism as a necessity, and this was bound to have some influence on any writing they did produce about it. As Robert Graves noted:

> [I]t is extremely unlikely that [a poet of the Second World War] will feel any qualms about the justice of the British cause or about the necessity of the war's continuance; so that, even if he has experienced the terrors of an air raid, he will not feel obliged to write horrifically about it, to draw attention to the evils of war. ('The Poets of World War Two', 312)

Outrage had been central to much Great War poetry, but the political climate surrounding the later conflicts made such outrage less conscionable. Revulsion against the whole affair would have been inappropriate.

All the same, though it was slower to emerge, the Second World War did inspire a lot of fine poetry, both at the time and afterwards – by the poets who fought in it and also by their counterparts on the home front. Much of the best poetry about the war was first published when the fighting stopped, as Douglas had predicted: whilst most of the war poets who survived the Great War did not write about it extensively in their subsequent poetry, many poets of the Second World War continued to write about it for a long time or, like Charles Causley and Louis Simpson, only published poems about war when the fighting was over. But a number of poets, many more than Douglas acknowledged or knew about, did write war poems at the time too. And the differences between the two world wars in fact often gave the poetry from the later conflict a thoroughly different set of resonances. As Alan Ross, a poet who served in the Royal Navy, put it: 'the issues of the war seemed clear beyond all ambiguity', allowing him to 'concentrate on recording a kind of existence as accurately as possible'.[6] And this is what Ross, Douglas, Causley, Simpson and many of the other poets discussed in this study were doing. Through their poems, we get a clear insight into day-to-day life at war. And we also get

3

poems about other aspects of a soldier's life that tended not to be subjects for poets in the earlier war, from the hunt for sexual gratification to evocations of the strangeness of foreign lands.

The label 'war poet' remains problematic and limiting, not least in a conflict that caused so much suffering among civilians as well as the military – and in which many of those charged to fight spent much of their time waiting instead. A lot of 'war' poems from the Second World War are essentially travel poems, about a strange sort of daily life as it was encountered whilst on service in far-off places. I have concentrated primarily, but not exclusively, on poets who served in the military in one guise or another between 1939 and 1945, and who wrote about their experiences in uniform, without limiting the study to a narrow focus on poems about battle and its closer corollaries. But this was a civilians' war too and, as the final chapter makes clear, the view from the Home Front is an important aspect of the poetry of the Second World War. I have also limited the focus to English-language poets, and as a result almost exclusively to poets who fought for or were resident in countries on the allied side. I hope that readers will not only find themselves inspired to read the work of poets included here, but also to undertake wider reading.[7] Ultimately, the intention of this introductory study is to draw attention to the often powerful poetry from what is, among readers and students of poetry, a largely neglected war, and to shed light on the diversity and inventiveness of poets writing about the Second World War as it appeared on land, at sea, in the air, at home, and in theatres of war throughout the world. This study provides a retort to that question 'Where were the war poets?' They were all over the place.

Something should be said about the choice of poets that have been given detailed treatment in this book. Other poets might well have been chosen. However, the present selection includes the two poets who really could not have been overlooked and adds to those a few notable others, all of whom were in the armed services but had utterly different experiences during what was, in effect, a war of wars. Keith Douglas and Alun Lewis served as officers in the British army, mainly in North Africa and the Indian subcontinent, respectively. Douglas engaged in and wrote about conflict, whereas Lewis died before his regiment was sent into combat, which explains why his war poetry is largely anticipatory and obsessed by strangeness. Charles Causley spent six years in the Royal Navy, working as a low-ranking coder on a destroyer. Unlike Douglas and Lewis, he survived, and continued to write powerfully about his experiences and those of his comrades. Randall Jarrell was in the United States Air Force, and served mainly as a navigation tower operator; he is, among other things, the finest English-language poet of the war in the air, despite not taking part in it himself. And Louis Simpson, a Jamaican-born American of Russian and Scottish descent, took part in the D-Day landings, fought across western Europe in the US Army from 1944, and wrote comfortless, vivid poems about what he saw. Their war poetries are as varied as their respective experiences of the war would suggest. Nonetheless, they can never add up to the whole story. The final chapter of this book explores many divergent representations of the war from other poets, both combatants and civilians, who experienced it. It is intended as a springboard for further reading, and to this end, a selective annotated bibliography is included at the back.

2

Keith Douglas

'The soldier who is going to die'

Until Faber and Faber published a selection of his poems in 1964, twenty years after his death, and then a *Collected Poems* two years later, Keith Douglas had been largely forgotten. Since that time, however, he has been widely anthologized and acclaimed: 'the one British poet of the Second World Was who can bear comparison with those of the First', as Michael Hamburger suggested in 1968.[1] It is a reputation based on a handful of remarkable poems completed near the end of his short life, but nonetheless a reputation that seems to have settled: he is for many critics *the* abiding poet of the Second World War.

Keith Castellain Douglas was born in 1920 in Royal Tunbridge Wells, Kent – quintessential middle England. He spent much of his early upbringing in the leafy village of Cranleigh, Surrey, and at six was sent to a prep school in Guildford, ten miles away. Douglas's father – also Keith – had been a military man of distinction in the Great War, and remained distant and aloof, but his son loved and admired him deeply, even 'emulating' him by playing at being a soldier in the garden and standing sentinel by the front door. However, by the time Douglas was eight his father had vanished from the household, not to be seen again. This must have had a profound effect on little Keith, of course, but his father's influence would be lasting: at eleven, he progressed to Christ's Hospital School, Sussex, where he would go on to join the school's Officer Training Corps (OTC) and become almost fanatical about drill. When he went up to Oxford, to read English, his extra-curricular interests remained military as well as literary: one minute he was with the mounted section of the OTC, which he joined at the first opportunity, and the next he was editing the university magazine *Cherwell*.

Douglas, then, was ready and willing when the inevitable war came, on 3rd September 1939. Within three days he had reported for duty, only to be told that because of his age he would not yet be called up. He was an intense young man, insecure, affectionate and pugnacious in turn; his two relationships at university both ended in his being left by young women who adored him but ultimately found him overbearing. But he felt cut out for war, and when his time to sign up did arrive the following year he entered training at Sandhurst, eventually joining the Second Derbyshire Yeomanry, with whom he was billeted at several places around England before setting sail for the Middle East in the summer of 1941.

He was perfectly clear-eyed about what this might mean, and even relished the prospect: 'I can see nothing more attractive than active service and final oblivion', he wrote before embarkation.[2] Indeed, as Ted Hughes has pointed out, 'Throughout his letters, and in the remarks remembered by his friends, as in his poems, recurs the cool note of certainty that he will be killed'.[3] However, after arriving in Palestine and joining the Sherwood Rangers Yeomanry – a cavalry unit – he was given a fairly safe job as a camouflage staff officer at Division HQ and reluctantly lived the life of relative comfort many others would have coveted. Eventually, after more than a year in the Middle East, first in Palestine and then Alexandria, Egypt, he could take it no more. Four days after the Battle of El Alamein began, in October 1942, he drove in defiance of orders to join his regiment on the front line. Rather than facing disciplinary proceedings, however, the following day he rolled into battle as a tank commander.

His desert war was brought to an end firstly by his walking into a tripwire four months later and being hospitalized for six weeks by the subsequent landmine explosion, and secondly by the German and Italian surrender in North Africa in May 1943. The summer and autumn of 1943 were comparatively leisurely for Douglas, but in December the regiment returned to England to prepare for the D-Day landings in Normandy. On 5th June 1944, he manoeuvred his tank past the initial Nazi barrage of mortars and mines and pushed inland, past Bayeux. Four days later, however, they once again came under fire. Douglas retreated to report to his seniors, and after he had climbed out of his tank to do so a shell exploded above him, killing him instantly. Like Edward Thomas twenty-seven years before him at Arras, no mark was found on his body.

A collection of Douglas's poems was not published in his lifetime. However, his adult life – and his poetry – can quite easily be split into geographically-defined segments, and this is how Desmond Graham divides his edition of Keith Douglas, *The Complete Poems*. After the juvenilia we have 'Oxford', 'Army: England', 'Army: Middle East' and 'England 1944'. It is clear that action stimulated his poetry as well as his spirit, and it is no surprise that the great majority of the poems we remember him for belong to the 'Middle East' section. However, Douglas was a precocious as well as a prodigious talent; his poetry reached a kind of maturity at Oxford and then developed rapidly. He wrote a number of accomplished and occasionally remarkable poems during his time there, and then when stationed in England, and though these poems date from a time when he was yet to see active service, his mind is not infrequently full of it.

This invigorates one of Douglas's earliest poems of real merit, 'Canoe', written in the leafy Oxford of May 1940, when he was still awaiting the call to fight. Here he makes clear his assumption that he will die on active service: 'Well, I am thinking this may be my last / summer', he writes with ill-fitting lassitude, the yet-to-come season pushed over the line-break, along with the intimation of a yet-to-come death (*TCP* 40). All the same, he 'cannot lose even a part of / pleasure in the old-fashioned art of / idleness', and 'cannot stand aghast // at whatever doom hovers in the background'. The repeated verbs seem on one hand to promise that the speaker is calm about his assumed fate, but also have a hint of imperative desperation: 'cannot' is not, after all, the same as 'do not'. The gentle setting, on the river as it meanders out of Oxford, is incongruous with such thoughts, and they are not dwelt on. Rather, the poem ends by addressing a lover, and looking forward to next year all the same:

> Whistle and I will hear
> and come another evening, when this boat
>
> travels with you alone towards Iffley:
> as you lie looking up for thunder again,

> this cool touch does not betoken rain;
> it is my spirit that kisses your mouth lightly.

This spectral return is fanciful in a manner Douglas typically eschews, even in his earlier poems. Like the repeated 'cannot' at the beginning, the end of the poem promises serenity but knows that the promise is not quite convincing.

A few months after writing this, when Douglas had become a cavalry trooper in the army, he left a typescript of poems with his tutor Edmund Blunden, one of the finest poets of the previous war.[4] Over the next year, he wrote several poems building on the preoccupation of 'Canoe', among them 'Time Eating'. Here he anthropomorphizes Time, which can bring a person 'to mansize from the bigness of a stone', but which also destroys: 'while he makes he eats' (TCP 71). As in 'Canoe', the speaker has an unerring certainty about his fate, if not when he is destined to meet it: 'though you brought me from a boy / you can make no more of me, only destroy'. He has reached a certain maturity.

These two poems seem almost to be brought together in the frequently-anthologized 'Simplify Me When I'm Dead', Douglas's last poem, and valedictory statement, before setting off for the Middle East. It begins:

> Remember me when I am dead
> and simplify me when I'm dead.
>
> As the processes of earth
> strip off the colour and the skin
> take the brown hair and blue eye
>
> and leave me simpler than at birth
> when hairless I came howling in
> as the moon came in the cold sky.
>
> (TCP 74)

We are implored to echo the process of time, of 'earth', on the body by paring back the speaker to his essentials. To emphasize the point, the opening couplet is repeated at the end, as the closing couplet. 'Canoe' seems to echo Rupert Brooke's famous sonnet of the First World War, 'The Soldier', and its consolation in possible death: 'If I should die, think only this of me: / That there's some corner of a foreign field / That is forever England'.[5] Douglas's last poem before departing for war turns the

9

probability of death to a certainty, and at the same time does away with all fanciful consolations.

The theme established in 'Time Eating' and 'Simplify Me When I'm Dead' would be picked up again in 'The Offensive 2', written in the winter of 1942–3 after Douglas had been involved in active combat for the first time:

> the sun officially goes round
> organising life: and all he's planned
> Time subtly eats.

> (*TCP* 98)

All is manufacture and destruction, one step forward and one step backward. The title of the poem recalls Wilfred Owen's 'Spring Offensive',[6] but whereas Owen's poem explores the various stages of battle, Douglas deals only with its anticipation, and offers little comfort: 'take as long as you like to find / all our successes and failures are similar', he writes, regardless what 'orators dropping down a curtain of rhetoric' would try to convince us.[7]

Another poem from Douglas's pre-combat period in the army, the astonishing and multi-faceted 'The Marvel', focuses on a close observation of what happens when Time eats. As with several of his most famous poems, which will be discussed later on, the poem looks inquiringly at a corpse. On this occasion the carcass under scrutiny is not human, but of a swordfish, 'spreadeagled' on a ship's deck (*TCP* 73). This is an intriguing choice of word for a wingless and limbless animal, implying it has been cut fully open, but one that also serves to highlight the comparison with Baudelaire's famous 'L'Albatros'. But rather than simply staring *at* this 'baron of the sea' (in 'L'Albatros' albatrosses are 'rois de l'azur', or 'kings of the sky'),[8] Douglas shows a sailor staring *with* it, in a sense becoming one with the animal he and his comrades have destroyed:

> A baron of the sea, the great tropic
> swordfish, spreadeagled on the thirsty deck
> where sailors killed him in the bright Pacific
>
> yielded to the sharp enquiring blade
> the eye which guided him and found his prey
> in the dim country where he was a lord;
> which is an instrument forged in semi-darkness

10

yet taken from the corpse of this strong traveller
becomes a powerful enlarging glass

reflecting the unusual sun's heat.
With it a sailor writes on the hot wood
the name of a harlot.

The beginning is thick with adjectives, each offering a surprise, sudden twist, or irreconcilable contrast: the swordfish belongs to the 'dim country' of the ocean – a place that, from our terrestrial perspective, appears as the 'bright Pacific'; the boat is at sea, but the deck, soaked only in 'unusual sun', is 'thirsty'. This foregrounds the poem's central contrast: the sailor demonstrates his dominion over this stately creature by using the lens of its eye for the function of writing a former paid-for lover's name into equally lifeless timber. It is a pathetic, lonely, doubly destructive act. The sailor sees only his past sexual 'conquest', but the lens he apparently unthinkingly uses to burn the name has filtered much more than the sun. The 'dim country' it belongs to is where sailors hope never to go, but often do:

... forgotten ships lie
with fishes going over the tall masts –
all this emerges from the burning eye.

He appears nonchalant; but the sailor's dominion over the fishes is short-lived, and perhaps due a reversal.

If the sailor is unaware of what, apart from searing heat, 'emerges from the burning eye' – and we cannot be sure that he is – we might think his lack of awareness is just as well. A comparable sense of being benighted underscores 'These Grasses, Ancient Enemies', written shortly before Douglas was appointed unwillingly to the relatively safe post of camouflage staff officer and when he would have expected to be sent straight into battle. The poem culminates by offering a perspective into the dehumanizing effect of war on participants. They 'meant / so well all winter but at last fell / unaccountably to killing in the spring' (*TCP* 87). Typically for Douglas, the poem passes no judgment: this is just how things are, perhaps necessarily. In the months after writing this poem, Douglas refined it into its shorter (and now better-known) variant, 'Syria'. The lines quoted above were among those that didn't make it into the revision, which ends instead with the soldier speaker, 'clothed / in the separative glass cloak / of strangeness', facing a chilling, cold-blooded animal that evokes comparisons to another – both of which are sinister counterparts to that marvellous swordfish:

> But from the grass, the inexorable lizard,
> the dart of hatred for all strangers finds
> in this armour, proof only against friends,
> breach after breach, and like the gnat is busy
> wounding the skin, leaving poison there.

(*TCP* 89)

Douglas's poetry is often informed by his strong sense of mortality, and even more so by chilling points of connection between life and death. Fish return in 'Mersa' and do what fish do:

> I see my feet like stones
> underwater. The logical little fish
> converge and nip the flesh
> imagining I am one of the dead.

(*TCP* 99)

Though it reminds him of his own mortality, this nipping is in fact harmless, and is in full view. The camouflage staff officer knew the value of remaining hidden, and in 'These Grasses, Ancient Enemies' and 'Syria', grass is an 'enemy' because it can 'conceal'. The earlier of those two poems calls Syria a 'two-faced country', those 'faces' being war and peace, as well as barrenness and abundance. Douglas's first year of active service may have been less active than he would have liked, but it certainly gave him the opportunity to travel in the Middle East, and what he found often left him feeling deeply estranged: he was more at home in a tank than in a souk. 'But among these Jews I am the Jew / outcast', he writes in 'Saturday Evening in Jerusalem', again using an enjambment for dramatic emphasis (*TCP* 112).

In several of Douglas's poems, from 'The Marvel' onwards, men are shown to seek release from estrangement and danger in pleasures – and sins – of the flesh. The namesake of 'Christodoulos', a brothel owner whose name happens to mean 'servant of Christ', is a profiteer from soldiers' loneliness and lust, who 'makes / God knows how much a week' (*TCP* 94). This, of course, is an ironic pun in what is a largely ironic poem. The seedy scene Christodoulos's services provide is presented in

12

such a way that we could almost be studying a battle zone, a place where flesh is rendered rather than pleasured:

> Out of Christodoulos' attic,
> Full of smoke and smells, emerge
> Soldiers like ants; with ants' erratic
> Gestures seek the pavement's verge.

The 'smoke and smells' might remind us, with another ironic jolt, of liturgy, in particular Catholic liturgy. However, these reeling soldiers are exhausted not by God's love, but by the thrilling but empty unlove that beleaguered the sailor in 'The Marvel' as he made burn marks of his own. Christodoulos's customers funnel out not as a human congregation, but like insects – so commonly a symbol or harbinger of death in Douglas's poems, from 'Syria' to the two great poems on which much of his reputation rests, '*Vergissmeinnicht*' and 'How to Kill', which will be discussed later in this chapter. They are dehumanized, but share with insects an inherent drive for what they find necessary.

The themes of foreign estrangement and wonder, bodily gratification, and death are returned to in 'Cairo Jag':

> Shall I get drunk or cut myself a piece of cake,
> a pasty Syrian with a few words of English
> or the Turk who says she is a princess – she dances
> apparently by levitation? Or Marcelle . . . .

> > (*TCP* 102)

'Cut myself a piece of cake' is 1940s army slang for choosing a prostitute, and the poem begins with a cornucopia of carnality. But the second and longest of the poem's three stanzas drowns this apparent escapism in a wash of inscrutable reality. Cairo is a 'stained white town' of 'legless beggars' and women offering their infants 'brown-paper breasts' that are 'elongated like the skull, / Holbein's signature' – an allusion to the anamorphic skull, a famous *memento mori*, in Hans Holbein's painting *The Ambassadors* (1533). In this second stanza, women are no longer objectified as readily-acquired objects of sexual gratification; breasts, in particular, are not sexually alluring, but are manifestations of time eating, providing nourishment and life whilst also foreshadowing death. The third stanza then moves outwards again:

But by a day's travelling you reach a new world
the vegetation is of iron
dead tanks, gun barrels split like celery
the metal brambles have no flowers or berries
and there are all sorts of manure, you can imagine
the dead themselves, their boots, clothes and possessions
clinging to the ground, a man with no head
has a packet of chocolate and a souvenir of Tripoli.

A 'jag', referred to in the title, is a 'spree' – and the connotations of this are given an ironic twist in these lines, where it pertains not to a bout of pleasure-seeking but to one of killing. This 'new world' is the warzone, an anti-pastoral scene where nature is mocked in the symbolically fruitless 'metal brambles' and the guns that are 'split like celery', and the quest for pleasure is mocked in the absurd, gratuitous yet quasi-comical final image of a headless man with some chocolate.

Douglas is in some senses comparable to Wilfred Owen. Both came to maturity as poets during their respective world wars and then were killed in action in their mid-twenties, and both are, by a small margin, the most celebrated and anthologized Anglophone poets of the conflicts in which they served. But the fact that Owen's most famous poem (and perhaps the most famous poem about war ever written) is the uncharacteristically shocking and visceral 'Dulce Et Decorum Est', should not prevent us from understanding that they are really very different poets. Owen tended to avoid focusing on the horrors of frontline combat, whereas in the poems he wrote during and after his service in a tank in North Africa, Douglas concentrated on scenes of horror with a coolness and relentlessness that might initially seem callous, even fetishistic. 'Cairo Jag' was one of the first of these coolly observed, disturbingly intense poems written after Douglas had experienced war for himself, but it certainly wasn't the last.

Douglas had a term for his technique: 'extrospective (if the word exists) [...] poetry seems to me the sort that has to be written just now, even if it is not attractive', he claimed in June 1943 (*PM* 121). The word in question means the opposite of introspective, concerned solely with examining what is outside oneself, and implies a poetry that is dispassionate, in the sense that it shows something in close-up without passing any moral judgment on it. That ending of 'Cairo Jag' might be called extrospective, and it is a technique the poet used to great advantage in many of his greatest poems of combat. But the earliest of Douglas's 'extrospective' poems about the cruelties of war, by several years, is 'Russians', written in 1940. This is the only poem of its kind that he completed before spending time in North Africa, and refers to an event connected to the Second World War that had made the headlines when Douglas was still at Oxford. In the Russian campaign against Finland of 1939–40, known as the Winter War, a regiment of soldiers had been discovered frozen to death, yet still apparently poised for battle. The twenty-year-old Douglas wrote up the scene as a neutral, articulate observer of the effects of war: 'Think of them as waxworks', he encourages us, before concluding: 'Well, / at least don't think what happens when it rains' – a final line certain to leave us doing exactly what it tells us not to do (*TCP* 37). This poem is in a sense separated from Douglas's other poems describing death in battle because of its geographical setting and the fact it does not relate to anything the poet could have seen for himself: it relies on reportage, not on experience, and for this reason he later disowned it. But it nevertheless establishes a method he would develop with great success.

The extrospection in Douglas's poems is typically combined with an unadorned poetic style quite different to the cadenced lyricism of early poems such as 'Canoe'. As he wrote from Palestine to a friend in August 1943:

> A lyric form and a lyric approach will do even less good than a journalese approach to the subjects we have to discuss now. I don't know if you have come across the word Bullshit – it is an army word and signifies humbug and unnecessary detail. It symbolizes what I think must be got rid of – the mass of irrelevancies, of 'attitudes', 'approaches', propaganda, ivory towers, etc., that stands between us and our problems and what we have to do about them.
>
> To write on the themes which have been concerning me lately in lyrical and abstract forms, would be immense bullshitting. In my early poems I wrote lyrically, as an innocent, because I was an innocent: I have (not surprisingly) fallen from that particular grace since then.[9]

In March 1943, a few months before writing this, Douglas had completed the poem 'Dead Men', an exercise in such unadorned concreteness. The 'dead men' are 'powdered' by the wind 'till they are like dolls', and the poem focuses on their potential fate with fitting objectivity: 'they tonight // rest in the sanitary earth perhaps / or where they died, no one has found them' (*TCP* 100). That first verb, highlighted by its position just beyond the interstanzaic enjambment, reminds us of what is perhaps our commonest euphemism for someone who has experienced the second verb. But as in 'Syria', or 'Mersa', no such dignity is afforded to men by the animals, by nature. Perhaps, rather than being left in 'sanitary earth',

> the wild dog
> discovered and exhumed a face or a leg
> for food: the human virtue round them
> is a vapour tasteless to a dog's chops.

'Dead Men' imagines the possible fate of soldiers who cannot be 'found'. Elsewhere, Douglas's extrospection is of a filmic, documentary variety. 'Landscape With Figures I' contrasts 'a pilot or angel' looking down on 'vehicles / squashed dead or still entire, stunned / like beetles', with those on terra firma who have come, 'like Thomas', to 'poke fingers in the wounds' of these metal cadavers, and who find that they are in fact 'disordered tomb[s]' (*TCP* 109). The Thomas alluded to in the poem is of course 'doubting Thomas', the apostle who would not believe the resurrected Jesus had appeared to the other apostles until he could inspect the wounds for himself: 'Jesus saith unto him, Thomas, because thou hast seen me, thou hast believed: blessed are they that have not seen, and yet have believed'.[10] In the context of the poem, this allusion implies that not having to look at such scenes of suffering is a kind of blessing, but by the time he wrote it in April 1943, Douglas had himself seen plenty of death and destruction: it was too late for that. In a letter to his editor containing drawings and watercolours he had made to accompany what he called his 'diary' of the campaign in North Africa (which was posthumously published under the name *Alamein to Zem Zem*), Douglas wrote the following note about one of his images. It suggests an easy acquaintance with such grotesque scenes:

> In the case of the man burning to death I have had to retain all the features, to give the chap some expression, although of course

they're expressionless, as their faces swell up like pumpkins. (*PM* 146–7)

Of course.

His most anthologized poem '*Vergissmeinnicht*', regarded at the time by Blunden as 'your best [poem] concerning present subjects', was completed in June that year. It takes as its subject a comparably hideous sight, and exactly the same kind of poking around he had described in 'Landscape with Figures I', whilst also developing the reflection in 'Dead Men' that corpses are 'less durable than the metal of a gun'. A soldier returns to a former battleground after three weeks, and comes across the decaying body of a German who had on that occasion 'hit my tank with one':

> Look. Here in the gunpit spoil
> the dishonoured picture of his girl
> who has put: *Steffi. Vergissmeinnicht*
> in a copybook gothic script.

> We see him almost with content,
> abased, and seeming to have paid
> and mocked at by his own equipment
> that's hard and good when he's decayed.

> But she would weep to see today
> how on his skin the swart flies move;
> the dust upon the paper eye
> and the burst stomach like a cave.

> (*TCP* 118)

This poem would seem to have been inspired by something Douglas witnessed in North Africa. In *Alamein to Zem Zem*, he describes stumbling upon a dead Libyan soldier: 'As I looked at him, a fly crawled up his cheek and across the dry pupil of his unblinking right eye. I saw that a pocket of dust had collected in the trough of the lower lid.'[11] The same event seems also to have inspired the description of a dead gunner at the heart of Douglas's short story 'The Little Red Mouth':

> It was like a carefully posed waxwork. He lay propped against one end of the pit, with his neck stretched back, mouth open, dust on his tongue. [...] A crowd of flies covered him: there were black congregations of them wherever the patches of blood were, and they were crawling on his face in ones and twos. (*PM* 140)

17

In *'Vergissmeinnicht'*, the soldier is a German – one of the arch-enemy, a Nazi conscript. The title is German for 'forget-me-not' – a word that, when applied to what a carcass is capable of, is as darkly ironic as that headless body in 'Cairo Jag' carrying a bar of chocolate. We are implored to 'Look' at him and join the speaker in an apparently incongruous state of near-content-ment, or fascination, as he pores over the vanquished enemy who would have done the same to him – who, indeed, tried to. And this 'looking' is complicated by the fact that we are cast as voyeurs, encouraged to imagine the dead man's lover's tearful reaction to something she will never see whilst ourselves studying the details.[12] The speaker remains apparently de-tached, inquisitive, a touch triumphant.

An insight into the emotional control Douglas exhibits here, at odds with the fundamentally emotive scene he describes, inheres in a criticism he made regarding the work of his poet friend J. C. Hall: 'I don't want that you should lose the sensitiveness, or even some of it. But that you should be deeply affected, and not show it so much' (*PM* 122). Unsurprisingly, though, some critics have found Douglas's apparent relish for macabre details a little hard to bear. John Carey, for example, claimed that *'Vergissmeinnicht'* 'edge[s] on disdain. The strictly rationed compunction makes the poem more distinctive, but less humane'.[13] But for all its extrospective coolness, the poem *does* humanize the enemy. We focus on what is just another dead young man with an apparently conventional but mean-ingful life at home: the senselessly degraded cadaver of a lad once capable of loving and still capable of being loved, who has been caught up in the machinations of a state and an epoch. He is one of us, a voiceless counterpart to the senselessly dead Germans populating poems of the First World War such as the 'enemy you killed, my friend' in Owen's 'Strange Meeting',[14] or the body propped against a tree that 'scowled and stunk', 'Dribbling black blood from nose and beard', in Robert Graves's 'A Dead Boche'.[15] The obvious evils of Fascism gave the allies of the Second World War a clearer sense of what they were fighting against than their earlier counterparts; but wars are fought primarily by ordinary folk caught up in others' ideologies, and Douglas understood this utterly. Rather than being dispassion-ate, then, poems such as *'Vergissmeinnicht'* hold up what might be a mirror as well as holding up a lens.

The poem ends by juxtaposing the two extremes of human nature, both symbolized by the corpse of this young man – who is recast suddenly as the bringer of death, as he might well have been, rather than its recipient:

> For here the lover and killer are mingled,
> who had one body and one heart.
> And death who had the soldier singled
> has done the lover mortal hurt.

The register soars as the poem reaches its climax, honouring the soldier and the 'dishonoured picture' of his girl, but also mocking his squalid corpse with rhetorical elevation in much the same way that the equipment 'mock[s]' him with its durability. But whilst the speaker can only be 'content' – this enemy cannot do the same to him – Douglas's reader is left to reflect on how little inherent difference there seems to be between this killed serviceman and those who finished his life.

Steffi, the absent and unseeing girlfriend in *'Vergissmein-nicht'*, provides a reminder that each dead soldier leaves a wake of grief behind him. 'How to Kill', written at around the same time, also emphasizes the wider sphere of loss, this time by alluding to a mother who knows her son's ways better than anyone but who cannot know, as we do, that he is being killed at that moment and so she will never observe them again. At first, the poem makes the connection between childhood play and adult war, as the 'child turns[s] into a man'. A boyish childhood is therefore shown to be a training ground for soldiering, and as with *'Vergissmeinnicht'*, 'How to Kill' implies an inherent pleasure, exceeding relief, in being killer not killed, hunter not hunted:

> Now in my dial of glass appears
> the soldier who is going to die.
> He smiles, and moves about in ways
> his mother knows, habits of his.
> The wires touch his face: I cry
> NOW. Death, like a familiar, hears
>
> and look, has made a man of dust
> of a man of flesh. This sorcery
> I do. Being damned, I am amused

19

> to see the centre of love diffused
> and the wave of love travel into vacancy.
> How easy it is to make a ghost.

That glimpse of motherly affection is reflected, sickeningly, not in any human 'touch', but in the *apparent* touch, from the gunner's point of view, of a crosshair on the son's face, followed by the terminal touch of ammunition. As in '*Vergissmeinnicht*', we are implored to 'look' at human death, and our moral sense is tested against that of the speaker as we do so. This is encapsulated in the enjambment 'I cry / NOW' and its pun on the verb, which pits the expected emotional response to the killing of somebody's son against the verbal cry of the gunner as he efficiently pulls his trigger on a moving target. But, the poem asserts, in order to learn 'how to kill', in order to master this ultimate art of war, one must become desensitized in this manner. And there is a hint also that the speaker understands the killer could easily have been the killed and the killed could easily have been the killer: there is no room for emotion when it could leave one to pay the ultimate price oneself. In a sense, then, the poem is both devoid of dangerous empathy but also implicitly empathetic, because the killer and killed are inter-twined in the same person, much like the mingled 'lover and killer' in '*Vergissmeinnicht*'. We know that the 'glass' is the gun-sight, of course, but the choice of word encourages us think also of a looking-glass, or mirror, as though he shoots his reflection – a man who could be him. The poem then ends with a simile for the closeness of life and death, in which a living being appears to confront an ethereal counterpart – not a reflection, but a shadow:

> The weightless mosquito touches
> her tiny shadow on the stone,
> and with how like, how infinite
> a lightness, man and shadow meet.

A 'weightless mosquito' touching 'her tiny shadow' might serve to remind us of our own inconsequentiality – how, as the end of the poem puts it, 'A shadow is a man / when the mosquito death approaches.'

The range of Douglas's poetry has been called into question: there is a lot of coolly observed pain and destruction in the best of his poems, so the charge goes, but not a lot of anything else. This now frequent criticism was articulated to the poet in a typically gentle letter from Blunden, written after he had seen 'How to Kill' and 'Aristocrats' for the first time in August 1943: 'I wonder if you are becoming a little pre-occupied with the dry Ironic' (*PM* 129). Perhaps he was – and he as good as acknowledged it himself in a letter he wrote to Hall shortly after completing these poems, on 26 June 1943: 'I am not likely to produce anything but virtual repetitions of [recent poems], until the war is cleared up now, because I doubt if I shall be confronted with any new horrors or any worse pain, short of being burnt up, which I am not likely to survive' (*PM* 123). Though a few months earlier he had interrupted his poem 'Desert Flowers' with the weary but over-modest assertion 'Rosenberg I only repeat what you were saying' (*TCP* 108),[16] Douglas was not one to write just for the sake of it, and indeed he completed only a small handful of poems between late June 1943 and his death almost a year later. One of the last of these, 'On a Return from Egypt', written shortly before the D-Day landings, looks both backwards at the desert war and forwards at whatever fortune might have in store:

> The next month, then, is a window
> and with a crash I'll split the glass.
> Behind it stands one I must kiss,
> person of love or death
> a person or a wraith,
> I fear what I shall find.

'Shall', not 'may': he is under no illusions. Perhaps this certainty in his own likely end is what enabled Douglas to write with such absorption and precision about the deaths of others: he mastered it by confronting it unshakeably. Here, though, he also signs off with an uncharacteristic note of fear – and, of course, he had been right to be afraid.

In February 1944, Douglas signed a contract for a collection of poems to be called *Bête Noire*, but following his death it was not brought to production. The poems he left behind, or at least the twenty or so of them that his reputation has come to rest on, are overwhelmingly in concert with the war-time philosophy he expressed to Hall in that famous letter of 10 August 1943: 'To trust anyone or to admit any hope of a better world is criminally foolish, as foolish as it is to stop working for it' (*TCP* 135). '*Vergissmeinnicht*', 'How to Kill' and other of Douglas's more celebrated poems offer no ostensible hope, or consolation, but they are poems trapped forever in the hard-to-stomach paradox of working for it anyway.

3

Alun Lewis

'We talked of girls, and dropping bombs on Rome'

Alun Lewis was born in 1915 and grew up near Aberdare, a mining town in South Wales. His three brothers worked in the local coal mines; Alun won awards to study for degrees, achievements that were anything but commonplace among people from his sort of background in the 1930s, and aimed for a career in journalism, but found work scarce and eventually followed his father into school teaching. This career was also cut short, by war, and he died on active service in Burma in 1944, four months before his twenty-ninth birthday, having suffered a self-inflicted and possibly accidental gunshot wound to the temple. He had recently completed his second book of poems, which, like the first, was written almost exclusively while its author was in the armed forces, and had enjoyed a period of literary success roughly as long as his time in the army.

Alun Lewis is often regarded alongside Keith Douglas as one of the two outstanding English-language 'war poets' of the Second World War. This might in part be because – unlike many of the other poets focused on in this book – the lives and literary careers of Lewis and Douglas share certain traits that in the public conscience link them inexorably and almost exclusively to that conflict. The war took their lives, but it also saw their poetry come of age, and was perhaps even the catalyst for its sudden maturity; like so many of the iconic poets of the First World War, such as Wilfred Owen and Isaac Rosenberg, their art was suddenly and greatly developed as a result of the event that would also curtail it. Of course, this also means that their poetry never had the chance to develop: Charles Causley, for example, also matured as a poet during and in part because of his service in the war and wrote about it extensively, but he lived on to the end of the twentieth century so we remember him also for his later poetic achievements with the ballad, religious poetry and children's verse.[1] Lewis, however, comes to us now as a poet defined by the war, whether he would have liked it or not – and as a rougher and less developed (if also more ambitious) talent than the younger Keith Douglas. As Ian Hamilton put it, maybe his verse could 'have found its best expression if [his] war-nerves had been allowed to heal'.[2]

Having studied at the University of Wales, Aberystwyth, and for an MA (by thesis) at the University of Manchester, Lewis returned to the Welsh valleys of his childhood, and his eventual teaching post was at a boys' school in Pengam. He became a permanent member of the school staff in November 1939, just a few weeks after the war had started. He was a committed and outspoken socialist, an unashamed idealist, a man who believed passionately in the virtues of education – and was also naturally impulsive. Despite feeling as though he would be unable to kill and claiming that 'I don't accept, in my soul, the implication of being British or believing in the League [of Nations]',[3] and despite flirting with the possibility of joining the merchant navy, he pre-empted any issuing of conscription papers by suddenly enlisting in the army in the summer of 1940, having passed a recruiting office and seen a poster calling for volunteer postal-clerks with the Royal Engineers. It seems on the face of it a rash decision, especially for a man with his essentially pacifistic ideals, and his reasons for it are complicated and unorthodox. The war was manifestly a just cause, at least in general. But Lewis was also a seeker of experience: perhaps he couldn't have done otherwise; certainly he approached the war as a test of character and an inspiration for his writing.

Soon after Lewis enlisted, his uncle sent him *The Collected Poems of Edward Thomas*, a book that resonated deeply with the young Welshman. At the time Lewis was stationed at Longmoor, Hampshire – just a few miles from the village of Steep, where Thomas had lived when he first started writing poetry at the outbreak of the Great War. A memorial stone to Thomas had quite recently been unveiled on the Shoulder of Mutton Hill above the village, and this became something of a pilgrimage site for Lewis in his spare time. The temperamental and circumstantial similarities between the two poets are manifold. Like Thomas, Lewis hankered after pastoral escape. Like Thomas, Lewis had enlisted to fight in war rather impulsively and for not entirely patriotic reasons: Thomas had been considering taking his family to America to join Robert Frost. And like Thomas – though in very different circumstances – Lewis turned emphatically to poetry just as his war began. Until that time, he had primarily been a writer of short fiction, but at Longmoor he embraced the 'pointilliste, spasmodic, spontaneous' form of poetry with a new enthusiasm.[4] As his biographer John Pikoulis notes, 'From the moment he had landed at Longmoor, he had begun to write with a new fluency and seriousness, indeed, may be said to have become a poet at last'.[5] He discovered Edward Thomas in earnest at precisely the time he found himself both on Thomas's home territory and in a distinctly comparable circumstance.

Two poems in particular, both written in the autumn of 1940 and among the earliest of Lewis's significant poetry, stem directly from his new-found infatuation with and empathy for Thomas. One is the four-part 'To Edward Thomas', subtitled 'On visiting the memorial stone above Steep in Hampshire': 'I doubt if much has changed since you came here / On your last leave; except the stone' (*CPAL* 29). This is a poem of modest, deferential understanding, barely mentioning either man's war directly:

> Climbing the steep path through the copse I knew
> My cares weighed heavily as yours, my gift
> Much less, my hope
> No more than yours.
> And like you I felt sensitive and somehow apart,
> Lonely and exalted by the friendship of the wind
> And the placid afternoon enfolding
> The dangerous future and the smile.

He shares everything with Thomas, save for his extraordinary 'gift': 'hope', 'cares', sensitivity, a 'lonely and exalted' separateness among the elements. The language is sedate, but this is undermined by the edginess of the heady enjambments in the first four lines with their two sudden lines of dimeter. 'Copse' reminds us of its macabre near-homonym (not least after the allusion to Thomas's 'last leave' and before that to the 'dangerous future' poet and subject both shared in their respective times), just as 'Steep' puns gently on the name of Thomas's village, emphasizing how name and location belong together. We again find ourselves rounding on what became of Thomas, and this adds significantly to the poem's underlying tensions when we consider not only the temperamental affinity Lewis feels with the earlier soldier-poet, but also the poem's later momentary contemplation of 'This war and yours'.

Another similarity between Lewis and Thomas is that, in the army, both spent a lot of time in England feeling bored and rained on before they saw active service overseas. The other of these two poems, 'All Day It Has Rained...', is a greater accomplishment. Indeed, it did a great deal to establish Lewis's name as a poet, and it remains his most famous piece of writing. The poem echoes Edward Thomas's 'Rain':

> Rain, midnight rain, nothing but the wild rain
> On this bleak hut, and solitude, and me
> Remembering again that I shall die
> And neither hear the rain nor give it thanks
> For washing me cleaner than I have been
> Since I was born into this solitude. ...[6]

Lewis's poem is split into two strophes, or sections, of twenty-four and seven lines respectively. The first focuses on the lassitude of the speaker and his fellow soldiers forced into idleness by the weather whilst training in the English moors, and the second turns back ultimately to a memory of climbing the 'Shoulder o' Mutton where Edward Thomas brooded long / On death and beauty' (CPAL 23).

Like the poem of Thomas's that it echoes, 'All Day It Has Rained...' emphasizes the attrition of rainfall by repeating the word 'rain', though in a far more drawn out, laconic manner. The poem begins:

> All day it has rained, and we on the edge of the moors
> Have sprawled in our bell-tents, moody and dull as boors,
> Groundsheets and blankets spread on the muddy ground
> And from the first grey wakening we have found
> No refuge from the skirmishing fine rain
> And the wind that made the canvas heave and flap
> And the taut wet guy-ropes ravel out and snap.
> All day the rain has glided, wave and mist and dream,
> Drenching the gorse and heather, a gossamer stream

Too light to stir the acorns that suddenly
Snatched from their cups by the wild south-westerly
Pattered against the tent and our upturned dreaming faces.

'Snap', at the end of the seventh line, seems to bring the description of the rain to an abrupt halt; but instead it pushes on, the next line beginning with a near repetition of the first clause and title of the poem. Eight of the poem's thirty-one lines – more than a quarter of them – begin with 'And', reinforcing the sense of attrition. And the sprawled-out, lethargic, syllable-heavy and assonantal pentameters not only capture perfectly the glum, repetitive nature of seemingly endless rain, but in so doing create a pathetic fallacy for the lassitude of this life in camp. The 'phoney war' had ended abruptly in May 1940, five months before the poem was written, with the German conquest of France, and by this time the war must have seemed anything but 'phoney': the Blitz had begun, and invasion seemed a distinct possibility. But for Lewis, stationed out at rural Longmoor, action was still not particularly close: 'Not a hint of War', he wrote to his parents at around the same time he finished the poem. 'I feel as if I've been cheated'.[7] The first line in the main strophe of the poem not to have an immediate rhyming (or half-rhyming) counterpart is the fifth, the rhyme not picked up again until the end of the section: 'but now it is the rain / Possesses us entirely, the twilight and the rain'. Dreary, subdued rain therefore bookends the poem's drawn-out, subdued present, the whole of the first and main stanza. Not a hint of war.

However, by the time we reach the statement that 'it is the rain / Possesses us entirely', we know this is not true. In particular, the poem has just claimed that

[...] we talked of girls, and dropping bombs on Rome
And thought of the quiet dead and the loud celebrities
Exhorting us to slaughter [...].

This is presented as reportage. However, there is a hint of scorn behind it, for the 'loud celebrities' who do not have to do the fighting themselves, if not for the soldiers talking of lust and killing in one euphemistic breath: 'girls' probably means 'sex'; 'dropping bombs' certainly means indiscriminate slaughter. It is a hideous pairing, if also a wonderfully natural one, emphasizing the unsorted nature of soldiers' chat in such circumstances.

27

It serves also to emphasize the sense-dulling properties of being a soldier, in addition to the sense-dulling properties of continual rain – and moreover, the choice of pronoun implicates the speaker. These are ideas that would obsess Lewis, and that he would develop in his later poems.

In the much shorter second stanza, the speaker turns from present concerns – or the lack of them – to remember what feels 'dearer or more to my heart' than anything else: the normalcy of children playing, and of innocent life going on as it should, with children

Shaking down burning chestnuts for the schoolyard's merry play,
Or the shaggy patient dog who followed me
By Sheet and Steep and up the wooded scree
To the Shoulder o' Mutton where Edward Thomas brooded long
On death and beauty – till a bullet stopped his song.

There is a discrepancy, of course, between Thomas's long brooding about 'death and beauty' and the soldiers' seemingly cursory thoughts regarding girls and Rome. But also very noticeable about this stanza is Lewis's apparent mistake regarding the death of a man he so admired: Thomas was in fact killed by a shell blast, his body left eerily unmarked. Ironically, a bullet would be responsible for stopping Lewis's 'song' three and a half years later.

Like Thomas, Lewis is a poet nourished by his home environment – in his case a loved but unlovely mining community in Wales, as evoked in 'The Mountain over Aberdare':

Our stubborn bankrupt village sprawled
In jaded dusk beneath its nameless hills;
The drab streets strung across the cwm,
Derelict workings, tips of slag [...].

(CPAL 87)

This place is far from beautiful, and is not in its prime either. But nonetheless it is cherishable because nearly gone; it belongs to a different age that can be valued all the more because it is essentially over. The 'colliers squatting on the ashtip' – detritus of mining that also suggests something gone out and beyond use – 'Listen to one who holds them still with tales'; but they are from 'a lost age'. 'Destruction' explores a similar theme:

Where my bread is earned my body must stay.
This village sinks drearily deeper
Into its sullen, hacked-out valley [...].

(CPAL 90)

This hacking out of the valley floor is 'Destruction' of one kind. But this poem puts the same landscape in the context of the war: 'now the impersonal drone of death / Trembles the throbbing night, the bombers swoop'. One kind of 'Destruction' has been superseded by another, of an altogether more estranging kind.

Lewis's second collection of poems, *Ha! Ha! Among the Trumpets: Poems in Transit*, is split into three sections: 'England' (already not quite home), 'The Voyage', and 'India'. As such, it enacts a journey from something close to a place of belonging, echoing Lewis's own wartime journey. Unsurprisingly, the estranging nature of going to war, of leaving home, is a leitmotif of the book. 'Before he sails a man may go on leave / To any place he likes', Lewis notes in 'On Embarkation', and 'most men seek the place where they were born. // For me it was a long slow day by train' *(CPAL* 115). But the book offers few moments of such respite.

The book's opening poem, 'Dawn on the East Coast', is set in a particularly uncanny location, for all of its Englishness. This is partly due to the native flatness and marginality of the specific part of the English 'East Coast' alluded to in the title – that of East Anglia – but also because this part of England bulges towards what was Nazi-occupied Europe and a central theatre of war, and sat at the middle of Britain's early warning radar defences. In November 1941, Lewis, by then a second lieutenant, joined the Sixth Battalion of the South Wales Borderers, stationed at Woodbridge in east Suffolk. He was also sent to the battle school at nearby Aldeburgh, and spent time guarding an RAF station at Bawdsey Quay, both on the fringes of the huge wetland around the River Alde and Orford. The poem vivifies these planar, outstretched, rather desolate surroundings:

From Orford Ness to Shingle Street
The grey disturbance spreads
Washing the icy seas off Deben Head.

(CPAL 97)

29

Orford Ness, a long shingle spit, had long been used by the military and had become a hive of army activity by the time war broke out; the oddly-named hamlet of Shingle Street, opposite the end of the peninsula, had formerly been a thriving settlement for fishermen and river pilots, but was cleared of civilians in 1940 to make way for the allied forces. This was a strange, sparsely populated area where wildlife flourished alongside harbingers of man-made destruction, where 'Gulls lift thin horny legs and step / Fastidiously among the rusted mines'. And here a dying soldier thinks not just of home and his sweetheart, but of the immaculate pleasure of easily-overlooked domestic normalcy: 'A girl laying his table with a white cloth'.

One of the finest poems in the collection, 'A Welsh Night', is a wartime poem from a very personal home front. A Welsh urban sprawl beneath Garth Mountain – so presumably Wales's capital and largest city, Cardiff – is 'huddled' between 'coal-tipped misty slopes' (*CPAL* 100). What goes on in its hidden houses is imperfect and impoverished, but also full of life and love: 'the streets / Hoard the hand-pressed human warmth / Of families round a soap-scrubbed table'. There is a hideous irony in the 'Munition girls with yellow hands / Clicking bone needles over khaki scarves' – the hands that by day assist in the effort to kill mend by night – but the poem catches them in the act of fixing and helping to make do. However, something beyond the material is missing from the lives of these people:

> A mother's chilblained fingers soft
> Upon the bald head of a suckling child,
> But no man in the house to clean the grate
> Or bolt the outside door or share the night.
> Yet everywhere through cracks of light
> Faint strokes of thoughtfulness feel out
> Into the throbbing night's malevolence,
> And turn its hurt to gentler ways.

This might seem sexist to us now, making assumptions about a man's role and a woman's limitations: can a woman not clean a grate or bolt a door? But we should remember the context in which Lewis was writing. During the war, when so many men were away on duty, a lot of women took up what was commonly regarded as men's work, in addition to performing all of their other duties, which is why the munitions girls of the poem work in heavy industry as well as being attendant mothers and housekeepers. The blacked-out urban huddle of homes with its hidden lives is a fragile stay against the 'malevolence' of the Luftwaffe; barely any light leaks from the windows, but where it does only love and 'thoughtfulness' is revealed. And the town is longing, it seems, for the safety of its men – and to welcome them, and with them normality, back again.

Death is not only the soldier's concern, of course. 'Death taps down every street / Familiar as the postman on his beat', as Lewis puts it aphoristically in one of his four poems titled 'Song' (*CPAL* 106), in what was perhaps the inspiration for the strikingly similar and now famous line by Philip Larkin: 'Postmen like doctors go from house to house'.[8] But, as 'Song' also emphasizes, a soldier's life is one in which death is always close at hand and the comforts of home seem further away than ever. And this is a circumstance that this poem also sees with specific sympathy for the wife at home:

> Oh lonely wife, Oh lonely wife,
> Before your lover left this life
> He took you in his gentle arms.
> How trivial then were Life's alarms.

This is a 'wife', not necessarily a widow: the poem doesn't make explicit whether 'this life' refers to the mortal coil, or to the more organic and human routines of home.

'In Hospital: Poona (1)', from the 'India' section, is a more explicitly personal exploration of these themes, apparently addressing the poet's wife Gweno. The speaker lies awake with his earthly cares, thinking of Wales and his 'Beloved', 'while the world / Turned its slow features to the moving deep / Of darkness' (*CPAL* 140). The 'darkness' is in one sense chilling and alien, magnificently unconcerned with him; but it also seems to bring the speaker and his love together, to eradicate the distance and differences between them. Knowing that his beloved is 'furled... in the same dark' means that

> ... sixty degrees of longitude beside
> Vanished as though a swan in ecstasy
> Had spanned the distance from your sleeping side.

> And like to swan or moon the whole of Wales
> Glided within the parish of my care:

31

> I saw the green tide leap on Cardigan,
> Your red yacht riding like a legend there ...

Note the verb 'saw' – not 'imagined' or something similar: this is as 'real' as a vision can be, when it *isn't* real. In this nocturnal daydream he is both gliding above his small homeland, a guardian amid 'the great mountains', and also with his love in the mining valley 'Whose slopes are scratched with streets', and where 'you lay waiting'. But just as they seem to become intimate, as 'My hot hands touched your white despondent shoulders', reality intervenes:

> – And then ten thousand miles of daylight grew
> Between us, and I heard the wild daws crake
> In India's starving throat; whereat I knew
> That Time upon the heart can break
> But love survives the venom of the snake.

This poem is an aubade, of sorts, a poem for lovers parting at dawn – albeit only in the heart-breaking, life-affirming imagination of the speaker. But this aubade comes with the final promise that love is as eternal as 'the moving deep / Of darkness' evoked in the opening stanza. It is rather more hopeful than the pained central stanza of 'The East', the final poem in *Raiders' Dawn*:

> Must
> Such aching
> Go to making
> Dust?

> (*CPAL* 94)

And this theme is picked up again in *Ha! Ha! Among the Trumpets*, in 'Water Music': 'What stays of the great battles? / Dust on the earth' (*CPAL* 137). 'Love' might survive even the venom of the snake, but our greatest human efforts – in war, for example – ultimately come to nothing.

The making of dust, and destruction of home, is a central theme of 'Threnody for a Starry Night', one of the longer and more ambitious poems in Lewis's first book. In Part III of the poem, Polish girls sing about how they 'cannot go back' home:

> We dare not meet
> The strangeness of our friendly street

32

Whose ruins lack
The clean porch, the shoe scraper,
The Jewboy selling the evening paper,
The bow-window with the canary,
The house with a new baby,
The corner where our sweethearts waited
While we combed our hair.
We cannot return there.

(*CPAL* 44)

The enjambment between 'meet' and 'The strangeness' is perfect, suggesting a coming-together and then denying it, much as the street would both be well known and, partly *because* of its former familiarity, now seem completely alien. The accumulation of detail moves us from the pavement, to the window, and finally inside, to new life, before reaching back outside to take in a snapshot of nascent, youthful love: the accretion presents an imperfect world of young potential that seems destined to blossom, though we know that it has now been reduced to rubble. At the foot of these details, 'We cannot return there' rings with finality, the second line of a neat rhyming couplet of trimeters – and indeed they cannot.

An abiding tendency of Lewis's, in both of his poetry collections, is to present a more natural, less affected (in both senses) world – of animals or civilians in one guise or another – carrying on its multifarious business in spite of and with no care for this man-made world of war and worry. 'The Peasants', from the 'India' section of *Ha! Ha! Among the Trumpets*, shows the current war to be a temporary condition and a curiosity, with another kind of purer life enduring aside from it:

Across scorched hills and trampled crops
The soldiers straggle by.
History staggers in their wake.
The peasants watch them die.

(*CPAL* 144)

This calls to mind Lewis's fellow Welsh poet R. S. Thomas, who was at the same time writing poems about rural labourers in Wales, referring to them as 'peasants', and showing them to be elemental and truthful in a way the speaker is not, 'enduring like a tree'.[9] The Indian peasants of this poem play a comparable

33

role. They are prototypes for humanity; they will endure when the soldiers are gone and their war is over. Here the soldiers are reduced to pitiful and unnatural curiosities. In the fifth section of the earlier 'Threnody for a Starry Night', they are equally doomed, and are presented as emotionally reduced versions of their natural selves:

> Now only beggars still go singing
> And birds in forests.
> We who are about
> A mass rearming for mass-martyrdom
> Are punctual and silent.

> (*CPAL* 45)

The birds (and beggars) go on singing. But, like the soldiers in the theatre of war, birds go on killing too. In 'From a Play', we are told that 'after the slaughter' kittiwakes and oystercatchers continued to fish – to conduct their own necessary slaughter – as 'We stood in the shadows, waiting events in Europe' (*CPAL* 41). And similarly, in 'The Assault Convoy', quieter and more elemental assaults go on: 'The hawk sees something stir among the trenches, / The field mouse hears the sigh of what survives' (*CPAL* 159). For this soldier at least, being inactive in wartime is especially hard because one's innate impulses cannot be dampened. Would that they could; as the first section of the two-part poem 'The Soldier' states, in a development of one theme of 'All Day It Has Rained . . .', such 'impotent impatience' is a 'dark cancer in my vitals' destined ultimately to result in 'disaster' (*CPAL* 24). But this is hardly an admirable or fortuitous state of affairs, and seems to go some way towards contradicting Lewis's earlier assertion, made in his local paper *The Aberdare Leader*, that he could not kill other people, either in close combat or remotely, by dropping bombs on them.[10] Moreover, there is an inherent discrepancy in the speaker's range of feeling and that which he ascribes to his comrades, buoyed as they are by vacuous pop culture: 'my fellow soldiers stroll among the trees. / The cheapest dance song utters all they feel'. The speaker is overwhelmed by 'Volcanic fires deep beneath the glacier'; these 'fellow soldiers' are alike only in aspect, and feel nothing – or at least not a great deal more than they might in a time of real as well as ostensible peace. He knows he has an atypically restless and brooding constitution which alienates him to a certain extent from his fellow soldiers almost as much as his role and circumstances alienate him from the beings, human and otherwise, who seem to pay little or no heed to the war at all.

However, Part II of 'The Soldier' suggests that something which is almost the apotheosis of indifference to human plights in this or any time – the flitting of finches in the trees that 'blossom / On branches of song' – is elemental and truthful in a way soldiers never can be. Moreover, observing them is calming. Their utilitarian, often vicious cycle of life

> Ignores the holy mystery
> Of boy and girl together
> Timelessly.
> Yet still
> I who am agonised by thought
> And war and love
> Grow calm again
> With watching
> The flash and play of finches
> Who are as beautiful
> And as indifferent to me
> As England is, this spring morning.

Of course, unlike the 'fellow soldiers' of Part I, *they* have no reason to care, and their beautiful, indifferent otherworldliness-within-this-world is the largest part of their attraction. They might lack the strength and wonder of the 'holy mystery' of human love, and moreover he may not concern them in the slightest, but they are the inadvertent and calming gift that allows Part 2 to have a so obviously less frenetic tone than Part I.

This is a theme Lewis explored again in '"Odi et Amo"', also included in *Raiders' Dawn*. This is an unsubtle poem (the title is the famous opening phrase of 'Catullus 85', meaning 'I hate and I love'), and there is a savage incongruity between the vileness of 'this blood-soaked forest of disease / Where wolfish men lie scorched and black / And corpses sag against the trees' and the constant need the speaker has for something greater or more persevering than anything awful that can happen to him or to anyone else:

> My soul cries out with love
> Of all that walk and swim and fly.

35

> From the mountains, from the sky,
> Out of the depths of the sea
> Love cries and cries in me.
>
> (*CPAL* 32)

Note the accumulation of details, from the deepest 'depths' to 'the sky', encompassing all fauna, and the repetition of phrases ('from the') and conjunctions that emphasize this abundance. The world is full, it seems, and the speaker needs only to love it, not to be loved by it: his soul 'cries out' with a need for the sustaining properties of giving love, not of receiving it. And remember that he is a soldier – charged, potentially, with eradicating part of that beauty.

This ambivalence is given a different complexion in 'Infantry', which suggests that soldiers pushed into hardship and mortal danger develop a heightened understanding of being. But also, paradoxically, their will to live is dulled:

> They learn the gambits of the soul,
> Think lightly of the themes of life and death,
> All mortal anguish shrunk into an ache
> Too nagging to be worth the catch of breath.
>
> (*CPAL* 103)

Such poems give weight to Lewis's assertion that 'I write always *against* the tug of war & the horror & tedium of it'.[11] The same might be said of 'After Dunkirk' – a title alluding to the evacuation of British and allied forces in Europe in May and June of 1940 – a poem which finds the soldier-poet burdened by

> ... thoughts that complicate
> What statesmen's speeches try to simplify;
> Horror of war, the ear half-catching
> Rumours of rape in crumbling towns;
> Love of mankind, impelling men
> To murder and to mutilate ....
>
> (*CPAL* 39)

To simplify also means to euphemize. That 'Love of mankind' in the abstract and general can inspire the 'murder' and 'mutilat[ion]' of *actual* men is manifestly repulsive, seemingly counterintuitive, and no doubt glossed over by the 'statesmen' who lead them towards – if not into – battle. What might come to mind here are Churchill's famous speeches of just that period, rallying-cries to a nation for whom all seemed on the verge of being lost; and if 'simplifying', perhaps necessarily so, in largely isolated Britain where many were ready to make a deal with Hitler and the very real evils of Nazism. All the same, even soldiers who survive the fighting (or withdrawal) risk a different sort of 'death' in a world that is an ostensibly macho half-reality, 'rough' and 'immediate', where 'the phallic bugle rules'. It is a world marked by 'rigid brute routine' that has the one virtue of 'making man / Less home-sick, fearful, proud', but which also makes him 'less a man' for all that. This is dehumanization, not emasculation. It is a dreadful price to pay, and is also paradoxical in perhaps the worst way possible: men are diminished by the fight for Man. As 'Threnody for a Starry Night' puts it, those 'rearming for mass-martyrdom / Are punctual and silent', and 'Where sweet eyes were / Now are hollow craters'.

In all of these poems, war itself is never far away, but 'Burma Casualty' is unusual among Lewis's poetry for presenting close up the physical as well as the emotional effects of warfare:

> And then a cough of bullets, a dusty cough
> Filleted all his thigh from knee to groin.
> The kick of it sucked his face into the wound.
> He crumpled, thinking 'Death'. But no, not yet.
>
> (*CPAL* 146)

The leg has to be amputated: '"Your leg must go. Okay?" the surgeon said'. The 'Okay?' is, of course, utterly pointless in practical terms, giving only the semblance of choice: it 'must' be 'Okay'. The whole grisly affair leaves the soldier still more dulled, no doubt out of necessity: 'He heard quite casually that his friends were dead, / His regiment too butchered to reform'. He is left lying 'in the lightness of the ward' and seduced by 'the dark'. Like the poet, he shares Rilke's acceptance of death, and his understanding that 'ultimately, and precisely in the deepest and most important matters, we are unspeakably alone'.[12]

The central themes of many of Lewis's poems discussed here are brought together in the four-part 'The Jungle', an unwieldy poem for all its fleeting moments of greatness, and the last one Lewis ever wrote. Soldiers come to a jungle pool to 'quench more than our thirst – ourselves' (*CPAL* 155) in a process that seems almost spiritual, as well as biological. But both the spiritual and biological are no more or less than needs, and the jungle is a place where one is constantly reminded that different creatures' needs are often mutually exclusive. In the first section, a 'crocodile slides from the ochre sand / And drives the great translucent fish / Under the boughs'. In the second, this is explored further. Back in the 'frightened continent', 'The best ones' – including those beside the jungle pool, presumably – are 'on some specious context gone'. They are busy seeing the world as it is, and the poet observes them with consummate detachment:

> But we who dream beside this jungle pool
> Prefer the instinctive rightness of the poised
> Pied kingfisher deep darting for a fish
> To all the banal rectitude of states,
> The dew-bright diamonds on a viper's back
> To the slow poison of a meaning lost
> And the vituperations of the just.

The disillusion and despondency is considerable; the epiphany, if this is what it is, is that everything is pursued for the existence of something else, and our human games of war do nothing to absolve us from that. Moreover, as he puts it in Part III, with 'we' perhaps more accurately meaning 'I', 'And though the state has enemies we know / The greater enmity within ourselves'. When at the end of the same section he sees 'The face distorted in a jungle pool / That drowns its image in a mort of leaves' rather than narcissism we are presented with an unheroic kind of tragic recognition, with 'mort' pointing both to death and to a surfeit of beautiful, necessary decay. This builds to the poem's final section, in which the 'killing arm' of the dehumanized soldier 'uncurls, strokes the soft moss'. They are 'ghosts', nothing more, in this place where death and life are at their most apparent and omnipresent. The poem ends with a meditation on how death might come, how the cycle might be completed, seeming to leave only two alternatives:

> And if the mute pads on the sand should lift
> Annihilating paws and strike us down
> Then would some unimportant death resound
> With the imprisoned music of the soul?
> And we become the world we could not change?

> Or does the will's long struggle end
> With the last kindness of a foe or friend?

This slew of unanswered, unanswerable questions at the end of the poem seems desperate, with the possible exception of the last, in which death is a 'kindness', a release from hurt and want, to match its necessity and beauty earlier in the poem.

Soon after writing these lines, it appears that the poet snatched his death away from friend and foe alike. One morning in Burma, just as it seemed he would finally see active combat, Lewis walked to the officers' latrines and was killed by a gunshot wound to the right temple from his own revolver; the gun was found in his hand. Meanwhile, back in Wales, his wife Gweno was editing the typescript of his second book. The army, eager not to sap morale, would go on to record a verdict of accidental death, but the evidence leading to that conclusion is slight. Many believe that his greatest gift as a writer was for fiction, and that had he lived we would remember him as much now for his prose as we do for his verse; certainly some of his stories, such as 'The Last Inspection' and 'Ward "O" 3(b)', are as polished and consistently convincing as any of the poems. However, he saw himself as a poet and the war turned him to poetry above all else. And his poetic corpus is extraordinary for its psychological maturity and ambition, even though few of the poems are fully realized in themselves.

4

Randall Jarrell

'For wars his life and half a world away'

Randall Jarrell is arguably the most influential American poet of the Second World War, and also one of the most moving, persuasive and original poets of aerial warfare. As David Perkins puts it, 'He expresses the pity and protest typical of the better poets of the First World War [...] but also a nexus of other feelings [which] persist'.[1] What makes it all the more intriguing is that he did so without taking part in any active combat whatsoever: Jarrell lived through both world wars and served in the second, but was never remotely close to where any of the action took place.

His youth was spent largely in Tennessee, where he was born in 1914, though the family moved to California the following year so that his father could run a photographer's studio. When Jarrell was ten his parents separated, and other than a year living with his paternal grandparents in Los Angeles, most of his adolescence was spent back in Tennessee with his mother. As a teenager his two obvious talents and passions were for tennis and literature, and from a young age his career ambitions were literary. After high school he studied at Vanderbilt University in Nashville, where he found himself in the company of men such as John Crowe Ransom, already a very well-known poet, and Robert Penn Warren, who was then a graduate student. Soon, with the help of these men, he had started publishing poems of his own.

Ransom, Warren, Allen Tate and others at Vanderbilt were associated with the Fugitives, and then with Agrarianism, both of which were cultural movements centred on Vanderbilt and rooted in Southern conservative political and social concerns.

Jarrell showed little interest in these social perspectives and more in those of Marx and of Auden, but Ransom in particular was a huge influence on him in other ways. When Ransom took a job in Ohio, at Kenyon College, Jarrell followed in order to work as his assistant. By this time Jarrell had already started to make a name for himself as a witty, astute and sometimes biting poetry critic, but his reputation as a poet was slower to develop. At Kenyon he continued to publish his poetry, which was at the time fashionably Audenesque, and also became friends with a young Robert Lowell. He then took a job at the University of Texas, and in 1940 married his first wife, Mackie. Then, two years later, his book of poems *Blood for a Stranger* was published by Harcourt, Brace and Co. His literary and academic career had taken off.

The next year, however, Jarrell became one of millions of new American recruits, following the US entry into the war after the Japanese attack on Pearl Harbor and Germany's subsequent declaration of war in December 1941. Jarrell joined the air force almost immediately, and initially trained as a pilot. He had for a long time been drawn to military aviation. As Lowell recalled:

> I remember sitting with him in 1938 on the hill of Kenyon College and listening to him analyse in cool technical detail the various rather minute ways in which the latest British planes were superior to their German equivalents. He then jokingly sketched out how a bombing raid might be made against the college.[2]

Not long after joining the air force, however, Jarrell failed an aptitude test for motion sickness. This barred him from becoming a pilot, and he was instead assigned to work as a celestial navigation tower operator at the Davis-Monthan Air Force Base in the desert of southern Arizona. It was a comparatively safe job, a long way from the theatres of war, though very closely connected to what happened in combat: Jarrell was partially responsible for the training that would keep his compatriots safe on bombing missions – and their targets anything but safe. As he described it to Allen Tate, in a letter, he ran 'a tower about forty feet high' where 'a fuselage like the front of a bomber is hung':

> The navigator ... sits in it, and navigates by shooting with his sextant the stars that are in a star dome above his head.... [W]e record his

41

fixes and other stuff, correct them if he's made mistakes, and so forth. (*LRJ* 121)

As John Lucas notes, Jarrell's war poetry is that 'of an outsider looking in, a commentator on the engagement with war of the others',[3] but he felt a great human, empathetic connection to those 'others'. His poem 'A Lullaby' begins 'For wars his life and half a world away / The soldier sells his family and days' (*CP* 169), and as he saw these men come and go he knew the sacrifices they were making as well as anyone, apart from they themselves, could. The war and his political and personal perspective on it gave Jarrell a subject and provoked him into writing about it in a flatter, more matter-of-fact style. The poems resulting from his experiences would form the bulk of his two collections *Little Friend, Little Friend* (1945) and *Losses* (1948), the books responsible for making him a celebrated poet of warfare.

Like many left-leaning Americans, Jarrell was wary of the impending war in Europe, and this wariness never entirely subsided. He thought deeply about the implications of and reasons for war and, though he empathized with his compatriots at Davis-Monthan, he was dismayed and disgusted by the motivations so many of them had for fighting. 'I get more political every year', he wrote in June 1943, before going on to state that '99 of 100 people in the army haven't the faintest idea what the war's about. Their two strongest motives are (a) nationalism ... and (b) race prejudice – they dislike Japanese in the same way, though not as much as, they dislike Negroes' (*LRJ* 103). Jarrell may have been letting off steam here, but it is certain that he cared passionately about humanity, and its collective survival and perseverance, and thought very deeply indeed about what the war was 'about' even if many of those around him did not. Moreover, he understood the implicit paradox, in broader humanistic terms, of training people so that they survive long enough to bomb generally innocent civilians, and his war poems are often at their most emotionally complex when he considers the contradictions brought about, directly and indirectly, by his role.

In 'Eighth Air Force' Jarrell refers to the men who fly missions for the US Air Force as 'murderers' and presents them at uneasy rest back in barracks: some 'murderers troop in yawning' while another lies awake 'counting missions' (*CP* 143). He only has one

42

to go before he is sent home – but, of course, that might be the one to kill him: as in Keith Douglas's 'How to Kill' and *'Vergissmeinnicht'*, the 'murderer' may well become the murdered.[4] That heavily charged epithet used to describe these utterly ordinary men highlights the fact that they are caught up in something much bigger than themselves, and not of their choosing. 'I find no fault in this just man', the poem ends, echoing Pilate's verdict on Jesus as reported in the Gospel of Luke.[5] Jesus was anything but a murderer, but this simple man's 'murdering' is State-ordered: he is a pawn of the State, the real murderer, whose victims are its henchmen as well as its enemies.

The influence of the State is central to Jarrell's most famous and most widely anthologized poem – and also one of his shortest – 'The Death of the Ball Turret Gunner':

> From my mother's sleep I fell into the State,
> And I hunched in its belly till my wet fur froze.
> Six miles from earth, loosed from its dream of life,
> I woke to black flak and the nightmare fighters.
> When I died they washed me out of the turret with a hose.

(CP 144)

Like the speaker of Charles Causley's 'Song of the Dying Gunner AA1',[6] Jarrell's poem is recounted by one who has been rendered eternally silent. We are therefore made aware that he could never *actually* communicate his story to us directly. Though his utterance is terse and laconic, the poem gives this silenced victim a voice. But that in turn highlights how people like him generally do not have one. The State removes these people, metaphorically asleep and unaware, from what is most natural, and delivers them into death.

For all its brevity and directness, this is in fact a deeply complex and allusive poem and deserves particularly close attention. First of all, if we are to have any hope of understanding it, we need to know what the title refers to. To this end, Jarrell provides his own note to go with his *Selected Poems*, as he does for several of his war poems:

A ball turret was a plexiglass sphere set into the belly of a B-17 or B-24 [bomber], and inhabited by two .50 calibre machine-guns and one man, a short small man. When this gunner tracked with his machine-guns a fighter attacking his bomber from below, he revolved with the turret; hunched upside-down in his little sphere, he looked like the foetus in the womb. (*CP* 8)

That last clause is a little fanciful, but the poem depends upon this point of comparison, where it is rendered with the quantum leap of metaphor. 'Mother' in the first line is both figurative and literal: Mother Earth, but also the individual mother. But this speaker does not address us from the human womb. Rather, he is – or was – in the 'belly' of an aeroplane, typically a vulnerable part of any body but not one associated (like the cockpit/head, say) with any control or self-determination.

The speaker, then, 'fell' like a child from one apparent mother to another, and that word also has rich connotations. Falling is not typically a positive or intended act. Moreover, the word evokes the biblical Fall, from innocence and perfection to experience and mortality. In the poem, the fall ends with a different kind of expulsion from Paradise in which the speaker is ejected into the new mother of the 'State', the capitalization of which implies this is the superimposition of the nation state rather than just the falling into a 'state' of mind or being. And whereas mothers typically love, and give life, nations have a habit of going to war and of taking life. In a telescoped narrative that jumps from birth to death and overlooks the individual life entirely, the dead gunner apparently fell straight from the mother, like a new-born from the womb, into the uncannily womb-like ball turret, a freezing and manifestly un-nourishing counterpart.

The State, for its part, is symbolized metonymically by the bomber, the vehicle of death, itself. And the human has been reduced not only from a man to a gunner – defined by what he kills (and is killed) with – but also to something animalistic. The 'wet fur' is the lining of his aviation jacket, soaked with sweat and frozen at altitude, but it is also semantically *his* fur, and as he wears it he 'hunch[es]': the predator gunner appears like – and is – an animal preyed *upon*.

Being six miles high puts the gunner between heaven and earth, between grounded life and ethereal death. But everything in the poem is confused: earth, and with it life, has become a dream, and the incoming fighters and anti-aircraft fire the reality. The 'mother's sleep', a metaphor for her false assumption of security, has rubbed off on the child, who only 'wakes' from it when transported to a point of no return in the belly of the State. His is an inescapable waking nightmare, the overwhelming soundtrack of which is the onomatopoeic internal rhyme of 'black flak' primed to kill him ('flak' is a corruption of the German *fliegerabwehrkanone*, or 'aircraft defence cannon'). As Richard Fein puts it, 'The gunner wakes only to know that he exists only to be a victim';[7] and those six miles prefigure that other cavity, six shorter imperial measurements in the contrary direction, from where he might narrate the poem.

The last line of the poem is as disgusting as it is laconic, the corpse evidently so mangled that a hose is needed to flush it out. The gunner dies in a place suggestive of birth, but the imagery here is more reminiscent of abortion, the body in this mechanical 'womb' of the State being ejected with pressurized water. The last line is linked by end-rhyme with the second, in which we saw the gunner hunched like a foetus in the belly of the aircraft/State; in the final rhyming partner line we see instead this foetal creature dead in the womb and then unceremoniously discharged from it.

The longer 'Losses', in the conflated voices of several dead airmen, is partially an expansive counterpart to 'The Death of the Ball Turret Gunner'. Though Jarrell's diction is typically straightforward in this poem, our understanding of it depends on us realizing that it splices a number of different speakers, and our ability to follow the shifts from one voice to another. In the first of the poem's two main stanzas, the focus is on a cadet killed before entering combat. He speaks also for his comrades, killed 'on the lines we never saw', 'Scattered on mountains fifty miles away', and so forth (*CP* 145). Shockingly, he admits they are so naïve and inexperienced that they have trouble finding words for what they 'had died like', beyond the deaths of 'aunts or pets or foreigners'. All the same, he expresses a shared sense of personal culpability, which seems also to result from State indoctrination: 'the rates rose, all because of us'.

In the second, longer stanza, the poem assumes the more embittered voice(s) of a composite of those killed in active service on missions from England, men who 'turned into replacements and woke up / One morning, over England, operational'. Between the two stanzas, we move from a voice of innocence to one of (relative) experience: as with the speaker of 'The Death of the Ball Turret Gunner', these recruits have 'woke[n]' into a reality of war, something their counterparts at the beginning of the poem did not go through. And the fact that they were 'replacements' tells its own grim story: each of them was only there because someone else had gone, and after their own deaths these replacements will have their replacements in turn. They have killed and been killed:

> In bombers named for girls, we burned
> The cities we had learned about in school –
> Till our lives wore out; our bodies lay among
> The people we had killed and never seen.
> When we lasted long enough they gave us medals;
> When we died they said, 'Our casualties were low'.

Killing is elided, mentioned only cursorily, or euphemized for those perpetrating it, in their sexed-up 'bombers named for girls'; when their own death comes, the State responsible for using them up will emphasize its low casualty rate – of no benefit to those who are among it. And when they are shot down over 'target' cities they have 'bombed' and 'burned', the bodies of those on both sides will be united in pointless death. The poem concludes with a quatrain that returns to the singular first person, which ends: 'the cities said to me: "Why are you dying? / We are satisfied, if you are; but why did I die?"' The question is left at the end for us to answer as best we can, for no answer is provided.

'The Range in the Desert' recalls the sort of places where the recruits in the first stanza of 'Losses' would have been stationed, and where Jarrell himself worked. The people on this range are presented as a motley crew of battle-wearied returnees and apparently ill-fitting neophytes:

> The wounded gunner, his missions done,
> Fired absently in the range's sun;
> And, chained with cartridges, the clerk
> Sat sweating at his war-time work.

(CP 176)

As these recruits shoot and bomb a desert in 'rehearsals of the raids', thousands of miles from any front line, the world immediately around them continues to be 'what it has been', as 'The lizard's tongue licks angrily / The shattered membranes of the fly'. In its comparison of war and the natural order the poem calls to mind sentiments expressed by Alun Lewis and Keith Douglas in poems such as, respectively, 'The Jungle' and 'Mersa', both discussed earlier in this book. However, the 'anger' Jarrell apportions to the lizard is strictly inaccurate: the lizard feels no emotion, it simply responds to circumstance, whereas people obviously can feel anger, and can be made to feel anger. The recruits practise the obliteration of cities, which many of them will carry out, in a stark landscape where the unsentimental nature of the non-human world is at its most evident. The men have come from various walks of life into an inhospitable, lizard-filled landscape. Here they learn to have something of the unsentimental nature of lizards themselves as they prepare to fight, as 'A Lullaby' puts it, 'for freedom and the State'.

As we have seen earlier in this book, many of Keith Douglas's finest war poems focus on observing and analysing corpses. Jarrell tends more often to focus on giving voices, directly or indirectly, to the dead, as can be seen in poems such as 'Losses' and 'The Death of the Ball Turret Gunner'. 'Pilots, Man Your Planes', on the other hand, takes an omniscient point of view to show the scale of one episode of carnage. This poem begins with pilots on an aircraft carrier heading for their aeroplanes in order to intercept a threat (the title is the command given over the communication system of the carrier), and ends with disaster. Aircraft have their wings 'snapped off' and 'somersault' to the water, and the fired-upon carrier burns and laboriously plunges 'home into the sea', leaving the survivors clinging to life on the surface:

> Destroyers curve in their long hunting arcs
> Through the dead of the carrier: the dazed, vomiting,
> Oil-blackened and fire-blistered, saved or dying men
> Cling with cramped shaking fingers to the lines
> Lowered from their old life . . . .

> (CP 156)

Now the 'dream of life', evoked in 'The Death of the Ball Turret Gunner', is above them, not below, and the survivors cling to the umbilical cord of a rope promising a link to a surrogate earth and with it the chance of survival. Many of them will die anyway. By focusing in this poem both on war in the air and at sea, Jarrell draws attention to how both take recruits out of their natural and innately survivable environment: these men fall and sink to their deaths, as well as dying from the fighting itself. Before it was destroyed, the runway atop the carrier resembled a 'road to nowhere', making 'nowhere' the sea and the sky. Now 'nowhere' is all they have left until – or unless – they are rescued.

With its tumultuous action, and its compressed present tense narrative, 'Pilots, Man Your Planes' is as disorienting as it is disquieting. 'A Front', also a present-tense narrative, provides a much slower accretion of details, and rather than one error or disaster unfolding on top of another without warning, the poem builds steadily to an inevitable-seeming climax. A front in warfare usually refers to the front line of fighting, a place of persistent danger. In this poem, however, the front in question is a weather front, a boundary between cool and warm air masses, associated with wind, rain, and sudden drops in temperature. The poem begins:

> Fog over the base: the beams ranging
> From the five towers pull home from the night
> The crews cold in fur, the bombers banging
> Like lost trucks down the levels of the ice.

> (CP 173)

The bombers are coming in to land, back 'home' from a mission. It is foggy and very cold, and the planes bang through frozen layers of precipitation as they descend towards the base. The vantage-point of the poem is from the base or close to it, so that as the first aeroplane lands it turns from a 'glow' in the sky 'suddenly to steel / And tires and turrets, huge in the trembling light'. From our perspective it comes into being, though this draws our attention inevitably to the fact that the 'glow' was an amorphous and vague identifier of something that is in fact very definite and concrete, a huge vehicle full of humans. The other planes behind it are unable to land: the next one 'pulls up with a wail', as though distressed, then joins most of the others as they 'drone southward through the steady rain' to land elsewhere. All seems momentarily to have been saved: the response of the crews and their guides in the control tower, communicating by radio, has been as steady and slick as the rain. However, 'one voice keeps on calling': one other bomber has a faulty radio, which allows it to transmit messages but not to receive them, so the control tower cannot give it any assistance. It 'gropes downward in its shaky orbit', identifiable only as a 'roar', and the poem culminates in its reunion with earth as 'the air quivers, and the east sky glows'.

Both planes which return to terra firma in this poem – the first and last – are first visually identified as a 'glow'. However, we ultimately see the successfully landed first aircraft in its full glory, whereas the end of the poem leaves us to imagine the condition of the other. The first aircraft behaved as it was supposed to – but so, in a sense, did the last, for we are told it followed an 'orbit', a constrained route. In other words, there is a suggestion that though the final event of the poem is a tragic accident, it is one that the plane was somehow destined to make. Moreover, the last action, though ghastly, is incongruously beautiful from the speaker's (and poem's) perspective, lighting the sky in the customary direction in which churches are oriented, the direction of the Holy Land. The title becomes an aural pun: this is an *af*front to our sense of propriety, not that we would necessarily want to get closer to the tragedy or see it from any other perspective.

The poems we have looked at thus far in this chapter concentrate on members of the US Air Force, some in training and others in active service. Jarrell shows a particular tendency towards making his war poems speak for those who have been killed in the service of the State. Though he understood the horrors of Fascism and the need to defeat it, the politically left-leaning Jarrell also saw the war through the eyes of those marginalized or undermined despite or because of it – even if, as in the case of most of the US servicemen he trained, he didn't think they understood the situation themselves.

The short poem 'New Georgia' in part considers another type of marginalization in the US at the time, through the lens of an American soldier. The poem is named after an island group in the Solomon Islands captured by the United States in 1943, and according to Jarrell's note to it the speaker is 'one of [the capturers], a negro' (*CP* 11).[8] He is a black citizen of a country where overt, legally-sanctioned racial segregation is the norm.

Racial segregation would in fact continue to be legal for another two and a half decades in much of the United States, and the Civil Rights Movement would not get underway in earnest until the mid-1950s – facts that are in the future of the poem, but that demonstrate how this inequality must have seemed a long way from coming to an end during the war years. The poem begins with him recalling feeling anything but free before the war: 'Sometimes as I woke, the branches beside the stars / Were to me, as I drowsed, the bars of my cell', it begins (*CP* 181). At other times, he 'moaned in sleep / With the stripes of beating'. But eventually the year came when he could be useful: not unlike the speaker of 'The Death of the Ball Turret Gunner', who 'fell into the State' from his 'mother's sleep' and 'woke' to a war, this man 'woke / To a world and a year that used me, when I had learned to obey'.

A sense of marginalization is also at the heart of 'O My Name It Is Sam Hall'. There are four human subjects in this poem:

> Three prisoners – the biggest black –
> And their one guard stand
> By the new bridge over the drainage ditch....

(*CP* 166)

This bridge has quite likely also been constructed by prison labour. As it is 'new', it might even have been completed by the prisoners in the poem on this very day. At any rate, as a location it provides the perfect metaphor for a poem emphasizing a point of connection, even of tacitly understood collective endeavour, between guards and prisoners. The poem's title is taken from an English folk song about a condemned criminal who is destined to be hanged – and who, like the speakers of several of Jarrell's war poems (though not this one), narrates from beyond the grave. In the poem, the four men have no choice but to listen to the military band 'Whose marches crackle each day at this hour / From the speakers'. But later, the guard starts singing '*Sam Hall* in his slow mountain voice' and 'They all' – so presumably the guard as well – 'stop and grin'. As Stephen Burt notes, 'Guard and prisoners hear the same public music, obey the same authorities, and finally resent them in the same way, setting their own private music against those impositions'.[9] And, of course, the choice of song is grimly ironic

– a manifestation, one might even say, of gallows humour.

'A Camp in the Prussian Forest' begins: 'I walk beside the prisoners to the road' (*CP* 167). This poem follows 'O My Name It Is Sam Hall' in Jarrell's *Complete Poems*, and we might momentarily be fooled into thinking that it will also go on to highlight a point of connection between prisoners and captors (unless the location provided in the title has given it away). However, immediately we learn that these prisoners are in fact 'Load on puffed load' of Jewish dead from a concentration camp that has only very recently been liberated by the allies:

> One year
> They sent a million here:
>
> Here men were drunk like water, burnt like wood.
> The fat of good
> And evil, the breast's star of hope
> Were rendered into soap.

The simple rhymes belie a rather more complex and horrifying truth, of course. The speaker, an allied soldier and liberator of the camp, paints a Star of David that he has 'sawed from yellow pine' and plants it for the dead. But around it, across this patch of forest, 'A filmy trash / Litters the black woods with the death / Of men'. This is ash from the crematoria, the ash of genocide, and as the ash coats the living trees beyond the camp a 'monstrous chimney' utters one last 'breath'. Breath is a sign of life: the camp 'lived' so that they might die.

The poem is guilty of saying little more than might be expected about the Holocaust (but what else is there to say?), and at the same time semantically overlooking the female half of the victims – though since the camps were segregated, it is perhaps fairer to note just that the poem is concentrating on a section for men. Moreover, the poem lacks the specificity of the remarkable poem to which it now seems comparable, 'More Light! More Light!' by Anthony Hecht, which is discussed in the final chapter of this book. But it should be remembered that the full horrors of the Holocaust had only recently become widely known when Jarrell composed this poem. He was responding, honestly and with typically restrained emotion, to the most hideous of all possible current affairs, not to history.

More successful is the shorter 'Protocols', set in the

extermination camp at Birkenau, or Auschwitz II, which was the biggest camp in the Auschwitz complex. This is another poem in which Jarrell gives a voice to dead victims, and here they are particularly tragic ones, for the poem is spoken by two casualties of genocide who were very young children. Throughout the poem they are differentiated by the use of italics for one of them, though otherwise are effectively indistinguishable in their comments as they report the things they experienced and that their mothers said to them during their ordeals. One remembers being squashed in a train that arrives at what he takes to be a factory with 'a smoke-stack', and the other recalls being transported on a barge from the Ukrainian city of Odessa, though both end up apparently sharing much the same fate:

> When I was tired my mother carried me.
> She said, 'Don't be afraid'. But I was only tired.
> *Where we went there is no more Odessa.*
> They had water in a pipe – like rain, but hot;
> *The water there is deeper than the world*
>
> *And I was tired and fell in in my sleep*
> *And the water drank me. That is what I think.*
> And I said to my mother, 'Now I'm washed and dried,'
> My mother hugged me, and it smelled like hay....

> (CP 193)

These dead children mirror one another in their simple statements, made using simple diction, and eventually repeat one another in the last line whilst seeming to address the fate of one another by reverting to the second person: '*And that is how you die.* And that is how you die.' Most shockingly of all, they are too innocent, too young, to realize much at all about what has happened to them, that they are victims who have paid the ultimate price in the biggest ideological mass killing in human history.

Much of the poem's strength derives from its bitter dramatic irony: the horror is implied without ever being stated, for the simple reason that the children do not know enough to state it. As a result, the poem cannot be anything other than understated, and this in turn leaves it to shock and appal with its incongruously bucolic and poetic imagery, as one child imagines he has been 'drunk' by water, and the other describes what we know to be the residue of cyanide from Zyklon B as smelling of nothing more sinister than hay – which apparently it does.

The central focus in Jarrell's poems about the Second World War is what he knew best and felt most personally responsible for. Most of his war poems – though as we have seen by no means all of them – therefore focus on aeroplanes and bombing crews, and though he did not experience what those crews experienced, he did share responsibility for their success or failure and heard about both directly. But Jarrell outlived the war by twenty years, and much of his finest poetry was written after the poems discussed in this chapter. The war gave him a subject, but it was only one of the first of many subjects for him. His later poems develop his interest in the marginalized and otherwise quiet, but after 1948 he would only very rarely return directly to the war as a subject for poetry. He also went on to publish several stories for children, and is remembered best of all as one of the most incisive, opinionated and entertaining poetry critics of the twentieth century. But he made his reputation as a poet largely because of his poetry from and about the Second World War, and it is a remarkable, if at times slightly repetitive, body of work.

5

Charles Causley

'Wounds or sea-water'

Charles Causley's life was affected very profoundly by both world wars. He was born in 1917 and grew up in Launceston, an inland town in Cornwall, close to the Devon border. The family were quite poor, especially after 1924 when Charles' father Stanley finally died from the effects of poison gas exposure in the trenches of the Great War. All the time Charles knew him, his father 'was a dying man. His service in France had shattered him physically. He was invalided out of the army in 1918 with a disability pension'.[1] It is hardly surprising, then, that when his own turn came to be conscripted, in 1940, he did his best to avoid the perils of army life in favour of the perils of navy life, and became a coder on HMS *Glory* – though the trench-war poetry of Siegfried Sassoon and Wilfred Owen, both of whom he had been reading since his teens, must also have weighed heavily on his mind.[2] It turned out to be a fortuitous decision, anyway, in terms of self-preservation: he never took part in serious military confrontation. But having suffered the devastation of war second-hand as a small child, through his father's slow demise, he now experienced it over a sustained period through the deaths of friends and peers. As we shall see, his war poems are often invigorated by tensions in wartime experience between comradeship and isolation, familiarity and strangeness, and feelings of guilt or at least anxiety about the luck of surviving.

By his own accounts, Causley did not take well to life at sea. In fact, he even seems to have viewed the sea as another sort of enemy. In 1975, when asked about what it had initially felt like to find himself in the navy, he replied: 'I was afraid. I was

54

seasick, and the sea was big. It was bloody big and much more frightening than the German submarines. My main concern was to stay on the thing and not fall over the side.'[3] He would forever profess 'a healthy distrust of the sea: of how it has affected my own life, and also how it has very determinedly ended the lives of some of my friends'.[4] Causley's war was not active in the sense that, say, Keith Douglas's was, but it was a long and often uncomfortable one, of anticipatory fear, redolent of family tragedy.

War was responsible for turning Causley to poetry as his primary means of literary expression. The young neophyte sailor had always been a keen writer, and had already written three plays, about lives and circumstances that he imagined to be more interesting than his own. But, as it had with Douglas's, being thrust into the theatre of war concentrated Causley's creative impulses: 'I think I became a working poet', he mused, 'the day I joined the destroyer *Eclipse* at Scapa Flow in 1940'.[5] Life in the wartime navy gave Causley both a subject of his own, and suggested the suitability of one genre above all others: 'poetry could be put together in one's head – when working at other jobs, lying half-asleep in a hammock, sitting in a bar – and written down complete, on a bit of paper the way a play or novel or short-story couldn't'.[6] The pocket-sized notebooks in which Causley made notes towards some of these early poems, and to which I shall return, are battered and bent, implying that they travelled with him, on his person. And whilst he did occasionally return to war as a poetic subject in his more advanced years, it is in his first two collections that Causley focuses most intensively on his time at sea and warfare more generally. With the exception of a few poems, his first short collection, *Farewell, Aggie Weston* (1951), is essentially a book about being a sailor in wartime, and the same is true of much of the second, *Survivor's Leave* (1953), with its grateful but unforgetting title. Often, the human subject of the poems grapples with being away from home, and being an ill-fitting military recruit; on the other hand, the poems about life beyond war are often poems of guilt and remorse.

From the very beginning, Causley, who had almost never left home, was taken a long way from it. His war initially removed him from Cornwall to Scapa Flow, the natural harbour in the centre of the Orkney Islands, almost as far as it is possible to go from Cornwall and still be in Britain; soon, he was thousands of miles further away still, as his ship sailed the oceans. This is significant in relation to the book title *Farewell, Aggie Weston*, the last two words of which are a slang term for the British seaport hostels founded by the philanthropist Dame Agnes Weston – 'something for which I have every reason to be profoundly grateful', as the poet put it.[7] Causley's book title is an apparent valediction to a temporary home-from-home on shore, a place of familiarity, as a ship sets sail. The only poem in the book to use the phrase, though, is 'Song of the Dying Gunner AA1', where it is uttered in the last of four ballad quatrains, seemingly by the spirit of the titular gunner – not before he dies, as the title would suggest, but afterwards. The poem's use of ballad stanzas, a form associated with narrative, belies the fact that this man's narrative has already come to an end:

> Farewell, Aggie Weston, the Barracks at Guz,
> Hang my tiddley suit on the door
> I'm sewn up neat in a canvas sheet
> And I shan't be home no more.

> (CCP 6)

The 'Dying Gunner' speaks the language of the regular conscript – like one of Kipling's soldiers in *Barrack-Room Ballads*.[8] He is a mid-twentieth-century sailor speaking to his comrades in slang they would understand. But Causley is careful to ensure that the naval slang does not pass the rest of us by. He provides gloss notes, telling his reader that 'Guz' is 'naval slang for Devonport', and that a 'tiddley suit' is 'a sailor's best shore-going uniform': speaker and poet would both have hoped to return to Causley's native West Country, at least temporarily. The speaker is, in every respect, a less fortunate counterpart to the poet.

'Song of the Dying Gunner AA1' reads, then, like a manifestation of Causley's fear, when away during wartime, that he might not see home again. Many other of his early poems take up that theme, and it had evidently preoccupied him long before he brought his first collection to completion. One of the pocket notebooks mentioned earlier contains what is apparently a squib:

> When I was in Gibraltar, Malta,
> Orkney, spiced Ceylon,
> What did I see when I shut my eyes
> And thought of home?[9]

This, at first glance, appears to be a tensely unanswered question – which might have been Causley's intention. But the answer 'Launceston' (pronounced 'Lanson' locally) would both allow the four lines to scan as another ballad quatrain, and provide a half-rhyme with 'Ceylon', linking home with the most exotic elsewhere it mentions. The four lines remain an abandoned fragment, but prefigure Causley's subsequent poetry about war and homesickness, in which a sense of human vulnerability and longing is often juxtaposed against exotic or eerily peaceful and beautiful surroundings.

'Conversation in Gibraltar' is largely given over to evoking the apprehensive inaction of sailors in port at Gibraltar. It begins: 'We sit here, talking of Barea and Lorca, / Meeting the iron eye of the Spanish clock' (*CCP* 17) – apparently watchful; from a country now neutral, but fascist. Gibraltar, ostensibly a tiny but British refuge from occupied and neutral Europe, is 'the profitable Rock', but 'profitable' things are fought over in wartime. Their situation is somewhat comparable to that of Arturo Barea, mentioned in the poem's opening line, a Spanish poet and journalist in exile in England and unable to return to his homeland.[10] In 'The Waste Land', T. S. Eliot draws attention to the detritus in a modern River Thames by evoking the sixteenth-century river which 'bears no empty bottles, sandwich papers, / Silk handkerchiefs, cardboard boxes, cigarette ends'.[11] Causley uses a similar rhetorical trick to emphasize what is in fact missing for these sailors but which they should have – what a better time would mean and the poem's present does not: 'We hold, in our pockets, no comfortable return tickets: / Only the future, gaping like some hideous fable.' And from the poem's perspective, poised with departure due to happen 'soon', that future might well prove hideous: between the ticketless comrades and their home lies neutral but unsympathetic Spain, occupied France and a sea hiding the U-boats of the *Kreigsmarine*.

'Shore Leave', from *Survivor's Leave*, expresses some of the same trepidations from the other end of a journey from home to elsewhere, pitting a desire to return to sea against fear for what that might bring. The very title of the poem hints at an anxiety: it is a temporary spell on terra firma, but shore leave is destined to be ended, once again, by leaving shore. Indeed, this is a poem obsessed by *not* being on shore leave any more. The opening line describes the moon, rather surreally, as 'a yellow landau' – a type of covered coach, and one named for a town in Germany. Even looking at the moon, then, is rendered into a flight of fancy that merges a means of transportation with a city inhabited by the wartime enemy, as if to imply everything beyond the speaker's present location is tempting but also dangerous. This is borne out later in the poem, in which he imagines sailors sleeping on ships out at sea and exclaims 'Would I were one!' But the poem closes by drawing attention to 'the unfaithful ocean / And the Siren's song', waiting to lure unwary sailors to their deaths. The poem is restive, even anxious. Neither going nor staying is satisfactory. And conscripted sailors have no choice about that anyway.

The speaker of 'Nelson Gardens', a poem named for a road and gardens close to the vast naval base at Devonport in Devon, describes being seduced into going to sea by a 'stroppy young seaman' who 'put his candid hand in mine': 'Come with me where the winking waters / Beam as bright as washing-day' (*CCP* 187). But a wink can belie a falsehood, and the speaker learns too late that the seductive comradeship is a sham: the water is 'Bitter', and life at sea alienating, for 'Though we sail the seas together / Each of us must sail alone'. This is an inversion comparable in effect to that in Robert Frost's 'The Tuft of Flowers': '"Men work together", I told him from the heart, / "Whether they work together or apart".' But Causley's poem is about having this realization in particularly bleak circumstances, and after being hoodwinked by a promise that is almost its opposite.

'Immunity' offers glimpses of comradely comfort on board ship, but these are ironic counterparts to the three types of enemy presented in the poem, the first of which is infectious disease: minute, impartial, and no less deadly than any war machine or nation state. The poem is mainly set aboard ship, somewhere just 'offshore' from Africa, in a climate so hot that sweat ran 'down to my ankles' (*CCP* 171). Causley's portrayal of the chaotic semi-order of naval procedures is witty and ironic:

the on-board 'quack' faints – after 'swallow[ing] his oath to Hippocrates', ironically – when he is supposed to be immunizing the speaker and the other 'naked sailors' with what is only referred to as 'jungle juice'. What he temporarily fails to immunize them with or against, specifically, is not stated, and this only adds to the sinister mystery. However, after spending time at Freetown and setting sail again, everyone on the ship seems mercifully to have dodged the dangers of 'Malaria, yellow and blackwater fever', and the sailors are exuberant. Their surroundings are wonderful, and they realize with apparent joy that, were it not for the war, their current experience would necessitate a glorious holiday beyond what many of them could afford: '"This could cost a fortune", we said, "in peace-time. / The sun so yellow and the sea so blue".' But this is hubristic folly, a literal calm before a metaphorical storm. A more conventional military enemy, and the alluring but equally deadly aquatic enemy, are waiting to vanquish them in the near future:

> And, for the record, off Kos a month later
> Where Hippocrates lived out his term,
> Most of them died of wounds or sea-water,
> Including the doctor. None of a germ.

The tone of 'Immunity' is broadly typical of Causley's war poems, which rarely display open anger at futility, or attempt to shock the reader with direct portrayals of violence, even though they are so often informed by a powerful sense of injustice and a veteran's understanding of carnage. 'Chief Petty Officer' is a case in point, for it so easily might have been underscored, even undermined, by rage. Rather, this poem is a particularly biting but witty satire of an emotionally inept non-commissioned officer who seems to share very little of the poet's humanitarian concern. It describes in some detail an isolated man with 'cruel ambitious eyes of almond' (*CCP* 14), this mixture of cruelty and ambition making it abundantly clear that his ambition is not of a gallant, preservationist kind. He is in another sense a 'petty' officer: far too enthusiastic about his responsibility, and the martial routines that a better humanity would not require. Evoking the carnage of one sea battle of the Great War, the Battle of Jutland, Causley imagines this officer as an eternal figure of

British military foolishness and imperviousness: a whole war later he will still be 'Waiting for tot-time, / His narrow forehead ruffled by the Jutland wind'.

For all its contempt, 'Chief Petty Officer' refuses this man the respect of inspiring anger, and instead subjects him to nothing more than wry ridicule. Of all Causley's war poems, only 'Soldier's Chorus', from *Survivor's Leave*, gives in to explicit rage:

> When the church goes up like the gasworks
> And the tower falls in flame
> Death will not tire of her fan of fire
> Nor worry who takes the blame.
>
> Say that you did it for glory
> Defending your hoary name
> It's still the same bloody old story
> And I'm pushed in the pit just the same.[12]

As with the references to Hippocrates in 'Immunity', there is a hideous irony here, with even the church unable to offer sanctuary to indiscriminate carnage. Linda Shires claims that 'Soldier's Chorus' might be 'the most direct anti-war statement'[13] in Second World War British poetry. But Causley omitted it from *Collected Poems* (1975). Possibly he worried that the poem might be construed as questioning the justification for war against Hitler, which was not a position he would ever have entertained. Also, though, the war poetry Causley chose to preserve was more nuanced. As I have noted in the Introduction, to be engaged in the British effort in the Second World War was to belong to a common cause with a justifiable central objective, which had not always been the case in the 1914–18/19 conflicts. This perhaps made it easier for the most part for Causley and his contemporary war poets to adjust without the same latent outrage to their roles and to the many aching estrangements inherent in life at war. There is no outrage at the motivations for war in any of the poems Causley preserved in his *Collected Poems*, only palpable if muted outrage at human suffering.

'HMS *Glory*', presents an impressively even-handed response to the deracinating effect of war. This poem's speaker is not human, but the eponymous aircraft carrier built in 1943, on which Causley served:

I was born on an Irish sea of eggs and porter,
I was born in Belfast, in the MacNeice country,
A child of Harland & Wolff in the iron forest,
My childbed a steel cradle slung from a gantry.

(*CCP* 7)

The ship has been 'born' in the Harland and Wolff shipyard, Belfast: we might be reminded of the most famous ship to come out of that port, RMS *Titanic*, and of her ultimate fate – after all, an anthropomorphized version of that ship could, at this point in the poem, have precisely the same story to tell. But this is a poem of long-felt and even whimsical nostalgia, as the ship recalls 'The lovely northern voices, the faces of the women, / The plane trees by the City Hall'. Like her sailors, on behalf of whom she appears to speak, she has been removed from her natural environment to the extent that rosy nostalgia seems an understandable emotional response. The poem is blatantly intertextual, its language and metre echoing Louis MacNeice's 'Carrickfergus', which begins: 'I was born in Belfast between the mountain and the gantries / To the hooting of lost sirens and the clang of trams.'[14] But this draws attention to the differences in what the two poems remember: whereas both are lavish in description, MacNeice's is not romanticized, as he recalls the Irish Quarter of Carrickfergus being 'a slum', and the brook running 'yellow from the factory stinking of chlorine'. Causley's poem has nothing to say about the dirt and despoliation of one of Britain's poorest and most troubled cities, nor the aftermath of the Belfast Blitz of 15 April 1941, which left nearly a quarter of its population homeless (a higher proportion than in any other UK city) just two years before, in the poem's phrase, the warship 'slid superbly out on the green lough'. The town behind it was in fact bomb-ravaged and poverty-stricken.

The phrase 'I remember' begins three of the five short stanzas of 'HMS *Glory*', so that the poem also recalls Thomas Hood's famously nostalgic 'I Remember, I Remember': 'I remember, I remember / The house where I was born'. In Causley's poem, just as in Hood's, the remembering is painful, drawing attention to the contrast between a happy then and an isolating, uncertain now. The ship's (and sailors') last memory of home is of 'Leaving the tiny cheering figures on the jetty for ever', and those last two words are chillingly ambiguous: are they hyperbole (a long

61

time can *seem* like an eternity), or grim prolepsis? In fact the ship would ultimately repatriate Japanese prisoners of war before returning home with her crew; but at the time the poem is set, that is all in the unknowable future.

So HMS *Glory* ultimately lived up to her name, and was a force against the estrangement of war. But it is more usual for Causley to consider war by addressing, in an equally restrained manner, the arbitrary deaths of others, and his own equally arbitrary survival. He certainly knew people who left to serve on the seas and did not come back. The blunt, short poem 'Convoy', for example, recalls a contemporary acquaintance, now 'under the blanket of ocean' with 'his eyes quarried by glittering fish', the sockets 'Staring through the freezing sea glass', as elsewhere ships 'Come sailing in' (*CCP* 13). There is an unstated hint of guilt that the poet has returned unscathed – returned, indeed, a poet – when death had arbitrarily taken away so many of his contemporaries. Regarding the subject of 'Convoy', the novelist Susan Hill, a friend of the poet, recalls him saying: 'I knew him all my life and then I came home and he didn't and I had to pass his mother every day in Launceston High Street. I always wished I'd turn to stone'.[15] Elsewhere, Causley stated that this event 'affected me more than anything else in those years', and claimed that 'from the moment I heard this news, I found myself haunted by the words in the twenty-fourth chapter of St Matthew: "Then shall two be in the field; the one shall be taken, and the other left". If my poetry is "about" anything, it is this' (*Poetry of War* 158).

One of Causley's finest and most celebrated poems, 'At the British War Cemetery, Bayeux', is certainly 'about' that. A decade after the Nazi surrender, the poet visited the orderly British war cemetery in France that gives the poem its name ('Afterword: Skylark' 190), not far from where Keith Douglas had been killed in action following the D-Day invasion of Normandy in 1944. The poem recalls his having walked where in 'shirts of earth five thousand lay':

> On your geometry of sleep
> The chestnut and the fir-tree fly,
> And lavender and marguerite
> Forge with their flowers an English sky.

(CCP 59)

This is almost a counterpart, albeit one starkly devoid of fervent glory, to Rupert Brooke's famous and fancifully patriotic poem of the First World War, 'The Soldier', with its 'corner of a foreign field / That is forever England [...] under an English heaven'.[16] Brooke's poem belongs to a naïve *Zeitgeist* two world wars earlier, though; Causley's poem is from a more knowing time, and by a poet who lived through war's realities. But even Causley's poem has something inherently whimsical about its portrayal of nationhood: what exactly *is* an 'English sky'? The fauna isn't exclusively English either, by any means, though all might be found in an English garden and chestnuts are common and celebrated trees in England. Moreover, its 'Englishness' is undermined by a proper noun: 'Bayeux' immediately calls to the English imagination not the glory of making an England elsewhere, but the Anglo-Saxon disaster of being conquered, as depicted in the Bayeux Tapestry. And unlike Brooke's imagined 'corner', the vast resting-place Causley evokes is overwhelming in its grotesque scale. No orderly 'geometry', no euphemism of 'sleep' and no sense of homely Englishness can alter that.

In the decade since the end of the Second World War, a new 'cold' war had arrived; but in many practical senses life in most of Europe had gone back to some sort of normality. By 1957, a rise in earnings and investment emboldened British Prime Minister Harold Macmillan to claim that 'most of our people have never had it so good'. At any rate, the speaker's world is in many senses utterly different from the one he shared with his comrades, men and women like the dead in this cemetery. At a loss, apparently ridden with survivor's guilt, he wants to offer them something: '"What gift"', I asked, "shall I bring now / Before I weep and turn away?"' Touchingly, though, it is apparently they who are able to shape a purpose for the speaker:

> *Take*, they replied, *the oak and laurel.*
> *Take our fortune of tears and live*
> *Like a spendthrift lover. All we ask*
> *Is the one gift you cannot give.*

In this personal epiphany vivified into a moment of spiritual connection, the speaker comes to terms with the way he must commemorate this field of dead, standing for so many other fields of dead: he must make the most of the way of life they died for; he must free himself from guilt. There is nothing else for it: all they want, after all, is the gift he cannot give them, the life he must not squander. To fail to observe their imperatives would be both a waste and an insult.

Unlike his compatriots Douglas and Lewis, Charles Causley was fortunate enough to live many decades beyond the war, but was also freighted with the moral guilt that such survival can entail. During the rest of his long life he became famous for writing popular ballad poems, and also for witty socially-conscious poems such as 'Timothy Winters' and 'I Saw a Jolly Hunter', often ostensibly written for children but equally popular among adults. His contribution to the poetry of the Second World War is very often overlooked, even though it is the most varied and, alongside Alan Ross's, the most nuanced body of English-language poetry to come from the War at Sea.

6

Louis Simpson

'Take this message back'

Like many American men of his generation, Louis Simpson's first experience of Europe was during the D-Day landings in June 1944. This experience would heavily inform his poems about the war, as well as much of the other poetry he wrote in the six and a half decades he lived after it. In 1944–5, he was a member of the 101st Airborne Division, a light infantry division of the US Army trained for air assault operations, and most of the time he served as a runner, responsible for transporting messages between officers and the front line. He then suffered a nervous breakdown, which affected him to the extent that he rarely spoke for much of the following year. After this, and quite slowly, he produced most of the war poems that helped to make his reputation, informed by his own experiences of conflict.

Simpson's first collection, *The Arrivistes* (1949), brought together poems written throughout the 1940s, and included many pieces concentrating on life at war. One of these, the disturbing short ballad 'Arm in Arm', begins with an image of corpses, 'both friend and foe', being piled up with machinery and hardware (*OH* 99). This image is echoed a few stanzas later, in a comparison of those buried in a churchyard and those digging in to stay alive around them:

> By a church we dug our holes,
> By tombstones and by cross.
> They were too shallow for our souls
> When the ground began to toss.

The dead may be at peace in their 'holes', oblivious, but the still-living are certainly not at peace in *theirs*. When a 'private found

65

a polished head / And took the skull to task // For spying on us' –
a deluded and intemperate counterpart to Hamlet's monologue
to the skull of Yorick on the vile finality of death[1] – it is hard to
see this as anything but the misprision of a man driven by
circumstance to madness.

The most celebrated and ambitious poem in *The Arrivistes*,
however, is the less straightforward ballad 'Carentan O
Carentan', named for a town just a few miles inland from the
Normandy coastline. Carentan was liberated by Simpson's 101st
Airborne Division, following the Normandy landings in June
1944, but only after the Battle of Carentan. Capturing the town
was of great strategic importance, allowing connection with
allied forces further east and providing a continuous allied front.
As a result, a fierce battle ensued from 10 until 12 June, often at
extremely close quarters, the Nazi troops occupying prepared
positions in and around the town. Many more allied soldiers
then died at the Battle of Bloody Gulch, a German counterattack
a mile from Carentan, on 13 June.

As John Lucas notes, though, the town's name is incon-
gruously 'reminiscent of some time-hallowed Romance. Cathay,
Hindustan, Constantinople.'[2] Certainly, the poem begins by
presenting it as a place of romance as well as Romance:

> Trees in the old days used to stand
> And shape a shady lane
> Where lovers wondered hand in hand
> Who came from Carentan.

> (*OH* 103)

But this is in the past tense. And at some time after the passage
of these lovers, it was 'we', the soldiers, who 'came two by two'.
Indeed, the formerly 'shady lane' may be a reference to what
came to be known to combatants and historians as 'Purple Heart
Lane', describing a route into Carentan on which many
American soldiers were attacked and killed on 9 and 10 June.[3]
Then, half way through the poem, the narration switches to the
immediacy of the present tense in order to recount an attack on
these soldiers. The present tense also helps to impart a strong
sense of panic, with the speaker alone when he needs guidance;
and the grisly details of death are highlighted through a series of
incongruous euphemisms:

Tell me, master-Sergeant,
The way to turn and shoot.
But the Sergeant's silent
Who taught me how to do it.

O Captain, show us quickly
Our place upon the map.
But the Captain's sickly
And taking a long nap.

Lieutenant, what's my duty,
My place in the platoon?
He too's a sleeping beauty,
Charmed by that strange tune.

(OH 104)

The repetition of sleep as a motif for death causes it to work against the typical principles of euphemism, encouraging us continually to reassess the aptitude of the metaphor. And after this, we reach that equally incongruous euphemism of that 'strange tune': a bullet, its 'tune' that so hideously 'charmed' the speaker being by definition 'strange' because death can only find you once. The poem ends by declaring that before they had come to Carentan, these men had not 'known what death can do'. They do now, even if one of them apparently cannot find the words to express it directly.

When Simpson's second book, *Good News of Death and Other Poems*, was published in 1955, he had completed his studies at Columbia, and was undertaking a scholarship at the University of Paris – no great distance from where his war had begun on the Normandy coast. This book again includes poems about his wartime experiences. 'Memories of a Lost War' recalls trudging in file, within earshot of guns, past 'burst boots and packs of teeth / That seem to smile' (OH 112). The image of corpses' teeth would recur in his long poem 'The Runner' (discussed later in this chapter) as a motif for uncanny lifelessness, as would the speaker's apparent lack of control over his behaviour: 'somebody says / "We're digging in"' notes the speaker of 'Memories of a Lost War', and that is therefore what he must do. The poem's title puts its narrative in the past, even though it is written in the present tense. Of course, this war was 'won', but the use of that word 'Loss' seems to emphasize that any first-hand experience of war is fundamentally about degrees of loss.

Good News includes the haunting 'The Battle'. This poem begins with that most familiar of scenarios for a war poem: a long and uncomfortable march, with a distant backdrop of dull carnage. In the first stanza we are told that, 'Like the circle of a throat / The night on every side was turning red': the battle is elsewhere, colouring the sky (*OH* 113). But, as this image implies in a foreshadowing of Simpson's later 'The Runner', it is also sickly and deeply claustrophobic. The marching men are rendered animalistic by necessity, trudging through trees before sinking 'like moles' by digging their way into burrows in 'the clammy earth'. Then it snows, and the feet of those on sentry duty 'begin to freeze'. It is a moment of clear understatement comparable to the relentless use of euphemisms in 'Carentan O Carentan', drawing attention to the horror by appearing almost blithely to pass over it.

In the third of the poem's four quatrains, we are told of the 'circle' closing in: a deadly conclusion to the throat simile at the start of the poem. In the morning, and then for 'many days', 'shells and bullets swept the icy woods', and in this ice and snow, among the trees, 'The corpses stiffened in their scarlet hoods'. Their moments of death – from cold or shell-fire we cannot quite be sure – are ignored, not lavished over. Ultimately, though, the cold of nature rather than the heat of battle claims them. Then, in the final quatrain, we learn that the speaker was present during all he has described (and has spared us from by not describing):

> Most clearly of that battle I remember
> The tiredness in eyes, how hands looked thin
> Around a cigarette, and the bright ember
> Would pulse with all the life there was within.

The survivors of battle were nearly dead too: emaciated, exhausted, 'all the life' within them being spent, symbolically, on an 'ember' and its attendant ashes.

'The Battle' is a fine and affecting poem, but it is also very conventionally a war poem, reminiscent of the tradition of English war poems from Owen and Sassoon to Douglas. However, Simpson is often regarded as a particularly American poet, and in some senses, his is a very American or American-centred sensibility indeed. He served in the US military, of course, and lived in America for almost all of his adult life; and in his later work – of which there is a considerable amount – American life and values are above all the central subjects of his critical, probing poetry, which would go on often to be written in Whitmanesque and distinctly 'American' long lines of organic-seeming and conversational free verse. But Simpson was born and grew up in Jamaica, to a Scottish father and a Russian mother (who was Jewish, which he found out in later teenage years): he only moved to America in 1940, at the age of seventeen. As he would put it in an interview:

> If I had not [joined the US Army], I don't think I would be an American writer at all in any real sense. Three intense years in the Army taught me an awful lot about being an American.[4]

So, Simpson's war poetry is predicated on the experiences of a man fighting for America, but who was also learning about it at the same time. This sense of being an outsider is fundamental to an appreciation of his early poems about the Second World War, and remains so in his later poems: he never entirely overcame it.

Much of this sense of estrangement seems to lie behind the long narrative poem 'The Runner', which was published in Simpson's third book *A Dream of Governors* in 1959 and which is dated at its end 'December 2, 1957'. A mini-epic in twelve sections, and arguably the greatest long poem in English to deal directly with life as a soldier in the Second World War, this poem apparently draws on the poet's own experiences in the US Army. The poem gives us no reason to suspect that the protagonist is anything other than thoroughly American in his upbringing, but he suffers different kinds of alienation whilst doing a job the author knew all too well in a place he knew all too well.

The poem begins with a prefatory note in which we learn that, like Simpson, the protagonist 'Dodd' is 'a soldier of the 101st Airborne Division of the Army of the United States'. The note goes on to stress that the poem is 'fiction', but also tells us that the fiction is 'based on ... history' (*OH* 133), specifically on a set of circumstances very much like those Simpson had encountered in France, Belgium and the Netherlands in late 1944, culminating in the 101st Airborne Division preparing for an attack by the Wehrmacht near Bastogne.

'The Runner' reveals a man desperate for acceptance: the

socially maligned and apparently socially awkward Dodd yearns to belong among his compatriot comrades. The poem begins with a rare instance of reported speech from the protagonist, a wry joke made after lunch and before scraping out his mess tin: 'And the condemned man ate a hearty meal' (*OH* 133). It is an ill-judged attempt at gallows humour, of course, and Dodd finds himself being told to 'dry up': 'Who needs your remarks?' (*OH* 134). His fellow soldiers do not want to be reminded of the fragility of their existence.

But Dodd realizes that, as much as his penchant for saying the wrong thing, education differentiates him from many of these men. Like Simpson, who suspended his studies at Columbia in order to join the army, Dodd has been to university. At one point he passes the corpse of 'Santelli, of the first platoon' – obviously a harrowing experience in itself, but also one that precipitates a memory of the living Santelli, who had once quizzed him, mockingly, on the reasons for the war and suffering. The third section ends with this recollection:

> 'Hey, runner-boy,' he said
> In the familiar and sneering tone
> That Dodd despised. 'What're we doin, hey?
> You've been to college, right?' his little eyes
> Were sharp with mockery – a little man
> Of pocketknives and combs. 'You ought to know.
> What's it all about?'

> (*OH* 140)

Dodd's answer is not provided – though what could it have been, in any case? The implication is that education cannot answer the questions that matter most. Moreover, Dodd finds that it cuts him off. Santelli may be dead, but his jibe evidently outlives him in Dodd's thoughts, and there are many Santellis left behind.

The poem's protagonist, then, is set apart from many of his comrades by education and social awkwardness, or a tendency towards unorthodox behaviour. But, even though he lives a life no safer and no less traumatic than anyone else, he is also looked down on by many of the soldiers he encounters by virtue of his wartime occupation:

> Now right here on this road,
> He might be killed by accident. But still,
> That wouldn't be the same as being brave.
> He had no chance to be thought so, no part
> In the society of riflemen.

(OH 144–5)

He is part of the supporting cast of war: if he dies, it will be arbitrary misfortune that kills him, not a chivalric misstep, such as that experienced by the loathsome Santelli, who went 'out in front' with his 'Rifle held crosswise' (*OH* 139). Of course, this whole train of thought (its twists and pitfalls occasionally, as here, emphasized through Simpson's light use of free indirect style) is the fallacious one of a psychologically weakened man. Dodd screams out internally to be a part of 'society', even a part of this society that mocks his learning and aspirations and disparages his character, but he could never find solace among this company anyway. It does not stop him feeding off scraps of compliments, such as 'You're a good man, Dodd': a throwaway comment uttered by a member of the mortar crew, but one which offers a crumb of hope for much-sought-after acceptance, and so leaves him 'Smiling, without a care' (*OH* 146).

Unfortunately for Dodd, his desperate bid for comradeship is dashed when he inadvertently disgraces himself whilst on a mission to deliver a message. Approaching a field he 'loathed to cross', where 'the dead were mixed as they had fallen' after a battle, he takes a path 'he did not know' and which he believes will lead him back to camp (*OH* 147). Incorrectly thinking he has stumbled into enemy territory, he runs away, drops his rifle and leaves it, and starts yelling the password, 'Ohio' (*OH* 148). It is an ironic password, of course, under the circumstances – for rather than taking him closer to his nation, blurting it out alienates him from his compatriots. His punishment is a mixture of time spent on particularly unpleasant menial tasks ('to dig latrines, / Pick cigarette butts up, scrub greasy pots') and overt alienation, as he is left 'to do nothing for a live-long day / But think and try to read, in a cold tent' (*OH* 149). Reading – learning – has served to alienate him already; now he would much rather be with his fellow soldiers, but is condemned to spend his time doing what he innately loves, within earshot of the men at drill and the corporal ordering them around with an insiders' joke: 'When I say Ohio, / To the rear march, and double-time like hell' (*OH* 149).

But much as he becomes loathed, Dodd also remains needed. Following his humiliation, the platoon comes under attack, and the last section of the poem closes with the first sergeant ordering the once again useful runner to deliver an 'urgent' message as the enemy appears to be closing in. The sergeant wishes him 'good luck!' – more, it seems, for his own sake than for Dodd's – and the poem ends:

> Dodd waved his hand, although it was too dark
> For the other to see him. And set off
> In what seemed to be the right direction.

(OH 161)

As John Lucas points out, 'The full stop where you might expect a comma after "to see him" is masterly', emphasizing as it does that he is 'now utterly on his own'.[5] Moreover, it highlights a parallel to the moment that precipitated Dodd's disgrace, when he previously set out in 'what seemed to be the right direction' on an unfamiliar route. This is his chance for some kind of redemption, perhaps; though it is clearly a tremendously dangerous mission and it is equally possible that he will instead become one of the dead. As we leave our protagonist in the dark, we are left in the metaphorical dark about his immediate future – a future more than thirteen years in the past by the time the poem was written.

The overwhelming impression of this comfortless narrative poem is of unbearable isolation amid potential companions – even exacerbated by proximity to them. Moreover, though we get to know him quite well, the poem's protagonist is repeatedly shorn of ostensible individuality: the title refers to him by duty, not by name, as is the case at many points throughout. We also rarely have the opportunity to read his direct speech, as exemplified in this snatch of would-be dialogue, in which we are given only the words uttered to him:

> 'Runner!'
>
> He answered.
>
> 'Take this message back.'

(OH 144)

Moreover, we are constantly reminded that Dodd has no real choice over his destiny: like the protagonist of 'Memories of a Lost War', as soon as he digs a hole in which to sleep, or settles, he is repeatedly being ordered to move on – and, compounding the indignity, in a solitary interjection of direct opinion, the speaker tells us that the men making the orders are 'morons' (*OH* 155).

The runner finds some solace in isolation, but this isolation also reminds him how foreign he is here. Near the beginning of the poem we learn that the American protagonist hopes to come back to western Europe, and specifically England, when happier times return: 'He liked the pubs, the mugs of mild-and-bitter, / And country lanes' (*OH* 135). Even the brutalized landscape of northern France fascinates him. One afternoon, after his disgrace, he walks away from the mockery of his fellow soldiers, climbs a slope, and sits alone under a tree:

> On the horizon
> Rheims, with the cathedral, like a ship
> Travelled the plain. Clouds were streaming over
> The spire; their swift shadows ran like waves.

(OH 151)

Amid the chaos of war, the deprivations and the sense of entrapment compounded by his isolation, he finds himself distantly overlooked by the huge and largely medieval cathedral of Rheims, a symbol of hope and faith more impressive and ancient than any comparable church he is familiar with from his homeland. Above its spire the clouds scud past freely, from somewhere else to somewhere else, with the apparent fluidity of waves[6]. It is a moment of sad peace, of contemplation:

> He lit a cigarette. Then, near at hand,
> He saw the earth was trenched. A long depression,
> No more than a foot deep, with rotten posts
> And scraps of wire, wound across the slope.
> . . .
>
>   He surmised
> This was a trench dug in the first Great War.
> Who knew? Perhaps an older war than that.

(OH 151)

This is no escape. Instead, Dodd notices the horrors of one world war are merely superimposed on those of the other. He is amid not only beacons of hope and salvation from the old world, but also layers of recent ungodly depravity over which this cathedral has also presided.

'The Runner' offers many points of comparison with other poems of war, some of which Simpson must have known by the time he worked on his poem in 1957. When we consider these points of comparison, it only increases the piece's inherent sense of comfortlessness and claustrophobia. In the second section, we are told that Dodd heard 'the familiar sound / Of guns' and then 'all his other days were like a dream. / This was the reality' (*OH* 138). Like the speaker of Randall Jarrell's 'The Death of the Ball Turret Gunner', he 'woke' into the 'reality' of war. But this is actually a *re*awakening for Dodd, for he has fought already, at Normandy: 'it seemed unjust / that he should be required to survive / again' (*OH* 138). The second enjambment only emphasizes the point that it is all happening for him a second time over. At a later stage in the poem, Dodd thinks he has been shot, and presumably believes for a brief moment that he will be invalided out of the army and sent home: 'He felt a sting between his shoulder blades. / I'm wounded, he thought, with a rush of joy'. We might be reminded of Siegfried Sassoon's 'slight wound' who 'lay smiling on the bed' in 'Died of Wounds'.[7] But Dodd has not been shot: his war will carry on, for the time being. Walking past the corpses of German soldiers, Dodd 'looked away' as 'A fly lit on the teeth' of one body – the opposite response to the inquisitive speaker in Keith Douglas's '*Vergissmeinnicht*': for all his joking about a condemned man eating a hearty meal, for all that he has woken into a 'reality', Dodd cannot in fact stand too much reality. And before he is sent out into the dark to meet his fate at the end of the poem, one of the last images is a long and distinctly 'extrospective' description of ice covering and even seeming to claim soldiers' corpses, 'clamp[ing] the dead in rigid attitudes' – an image that brings to mind Douglas's comfortless and disturbing poem 'Russians' – just before we see Simpson's protagonist going out alone into the dark with every likelihood of experiencing a similar fate.[8]

'The Runner' is in fairly loose blank verse: it is less metrically strict than most of Simpson's war poems and also differs from a lot of them by not employing rhyme, which gives the lines a freedom closer to prose. Simpson's next collection was *The End of*

the Road (1963), which won him the Pulitzer Prize. It also marked
a clear stylistic departure for the poet, to a looser free verse
somewhat reminiscent of Walt Whitman, and of Allen Ginsberg,
whom Simpson had come to admire. This allowed Simpson to
adopt an even more organic, conversational tone, whilst saying
the almost unsayable. 'A Story About Chicken Soup' breaks with
propriety to speak the truth about a family:

> But the Germans killed them.
> I know it's in bad taste to say it,
> But it's true. The Germans killed them all.

> (OH 182)

The focus of most of the poems in this book is closer to home,
though. Like Ginsberg, up to a point, Simpson is deeply critical
of aspects of American life. Moreover, he maintained something
of the perspective of an outsider in that country. As he put it a
decade later,

> I think that I have been inventing a United States, because I came to
> it from the outside.... Now that has certain advantages. It means
> that I will look at a character and think 'How strange', when nobody
> else would look at him twice. Or I would look at a scene in a street or
> something and think 'How odd' and 'These Americans!', you know?
> And think in those terms when they themselves don't see it. ('A
> Conversation' 101)

The End of the Road is particularly well known for its often ironic
and at times excoriating attack on American values, and it also
continues to draw on experiences of and reflections on war.

Both appear central to 'On the Lawn at the Villa'. Simpson
was at this time beginning to question the US involvement in
Vietnam, but the war in question in the poem remains
unnamed. The poem begins in a somewhat passive-aggressive,
wholly metapoetic vein, cajoling the reader into agreeing with
something it is made clear they shouldn't:

> On the lawn at the villa –
> That's the way to start, eh, reader?
> We know where we stand – somewhere expensive....

> (OH 191)

The people on this lawn, including 'a manufacturer of
explosives', are not especially admirable; but the speaker, 'being

American', is 'Willing to talk to these malefactors' whilst also believing himself to be 'somehow superior'. Of course, he might strike us as no different from them at all. That poem ends with the surreal image of dead killers from an unnamed war, brought shockingly into the genteel present of this man relaxing on the lawn – a killer who never has to come face to face with the human results of his trade – and his relentlessly passive companions:

> We were all sitting there paralysed
> In the hot Tuscan afternoon,
> And the bodies of the machine-gun crew were draped over
>   the balcony.

The men and women on the lawn are 'paralysed' by sun; the paralysis of the dead crew, obtrusively drawn out in that over-long final line, is less metaphorical. The genteel loungers of the present somehow do not seem to notice what has happened here. But for Simpson, who had seen so much of war in a relatively short time, such decimations were not so easy to overlook or forget.

This is the subject of 'American Dreams', published in 1971. Here, Simpson's outsider's perspective on American life precipitates a startling observation on war, and as Grevel Lindop points out, he writes 'about Vietnam through [his] own lingering post-traumatic stress'.[9] The speaker, a resident of California and apparently far from any front of war, imagines his world transported into a battle-zone reminiscent not only of parts of Vietnam, but also of the north-western Europe he had encountered near the end of the Second World War:

> As I look down the street
> on a typical sunny day in California
> it is my house that is burning
> and my dear ones that lie in the gutter
> as the American army enters.

> (*OH* 219)

The emphasis in the third and fourth lines of this stanza should perhaps be on the repeated pronouns, rather than the nouns following them: the poem stresses that Americans are used to the victims being someone else, somewhere else.

Long after Vietnam, even as the Cold War came to an end,

Simpson continued to be drawn to thoughts of the Second World War. 'Sea of Grass', published in 1990, is a case in point. The poem is an elegy dedicated to the memory of the painter Jimmy Ernst (1920–84), the son of Max Ernst, who had fled Germany for New York in 1938. During the war, his mother Luise was imprisoned at Auschwitz and did not survive, and the poem largely focuses on this:

> At Auschwitz shortly before the end
> one had seen her: 'a woman totally exhausted,
> half lying, half leaning against a wall,
> warming herself in the last rays of a dying sun.'
>
> And still we believe in loving-kindness.

(OH 357)

But Simpson then turns from this comfortless past to the present, and to a polluted shore of 'litter' and 'plastic bottles' near the speaker's home. The dedicatee, we learn, looked past this detritus to the 'Sea of Grass' beyond it. In spite of any amount of waste, the vegetation continues its annual renewal:

> There they are every summer
> just as he painted them,
> growing up again ... a hedge
> of stems and leaves standing motionless.
>
> Blue water, and a harbor's mouth
> opening into the sky.

(OH 358)

If there is to be any solace in a world of deprivations, it is perhaps best looked for by seeing beyond ourselves, and our present.

7

Naming of Parts: Some Other Poets of the Second World War

The five poets considered thus far in this study testify to the vitality of some of the poetry written by those serving in the military between 1939 and 1945. But there is great breadth to the Anglophone poetry written by those directly affected by the Second World War. This should not be surprising, of course: it was fought on many more fronts than any other war in human history; advancements in military technology meant it was also much more of a global civilians' war than the Great War had been; and a large chunk of the Anglophone world – the USA – was far more involved, and for considerably longer, than it had been in that earlier war. This chapter provides an overview of some of the other rich and varied English-language poetry from and about the Second World War.

Louis Simpson and Charles Causley wrote most memorably of war only after they had come home. And perhaps, for all their brilliance, the war killed both Keith Douglas and Alun Lewis before either had written what would have been his finest poetry. Spare a thought, then, for Drummond Allison and Sidney Keyes, two poets who met in wartime Oxford, and who were both killed in action in 1943 at the even younger ages of twenty-two and twenty, respectively. Had they lived it is possible we might now talk about them – or at least about Keyes – in the same breath as Douglas and Lewis.

Allison went up to Oxford from Bishop Stortford College, a minor public school, almost at the same time Hitler invaded Poland. Initially, he was a pacifist; this changed when he came to understand something of the true nature of Nazism, but still he managed to put off conscription until 1943 – the same year that his only collection of poems, *The Yellow Night*, was published. His war began in Italy that October, at the Battle of Monte Cassino, and ended less than two weeks later when he was killed in action.

His poetry has its admirers, among them Geoffrey Hill and Anthony Thwaite, and has been the subject of a complimentary biography by Ross Davies, published in 2009. However, his work is largely derivative: he emulated the rhythms and constructions of Dylan Thomas one minute, Auden and MacNeice the next, and died before finding out quite what he sounded like himself. His best remembered poem, 'Come, Let Us Pity Death', personifies death in a manner that calls to mind a little too readily John Donne's 'Holy Sonnet X' ('Death, be not proud').[1] Allison pitches Death as the relentless killer – but this killer is to be pitied rather than reviled for he knows nothing of the human joys preceding the inevitable moment:

> Come, let us pity not the dead but Death
> For He can only come when we are leaving,
> He cannot stay for tea or share our sherry.
> He makes the old man vomit on the hearthrug
> But never knew his heart before it failed him.
> He shoves the shopgirl under the curt lorry
> But could not watch her body undivided.[2]

This is far from perfect – in fact, the bathos of line three renders it straightforwardly risible. But the poem has its linguistic turns of genuine finesse, such as the double resonance of 'heart' as both a reference to the bodily organ and a metaphor for the man's humanity, and the stilting, exacting, unstressed line endings. The poem's central shock, however, is reserved for the two lines following the passage quoted above: 'Swerving the cannon-shell to smash the airman / He had no time to hear my brother laughing'. The speaker's brother is among Death's victims – and indeed Allison's brother had died earlier in the war when the bomber he was piloting had been shot down over Germany. The poem is defiant, full of zest and devoid of mourning: 'Come, let us pity Death but not the dead', it ends. But it is also a poem of faith in humanity: Allison knew when he wrote this that he would inevitably fight and might die, but he refused to blame the military enemy. Death is responsible, whatever clothes he wears.

Sidney Keyes was both younger and a more accomplished poet. He shares with his friend the fate of having been killed in action within a fortnight of deployment (in Keyes's case, in Tunisia), and none of the poems he is said to have written during his brief armed service have survived. As such, he comes to us a poet of apprehension, not of experienced action. In the short essay 'Poets of This War' (1943), written just after Keyes's death but without any knowledge of it, Keith Douglas described Keyes as 'technically quite competent' but with 'no experiences worth writing of' (*PM* 119). But Keyes turned his attention elsewhere, and his erudition helped him to see the war he was destined to join in its historical context.

His long poem 'The Foreign Gate', written in the winter of 1941–2, considers wars through the panoramic lens of history. The speaker offers to act as a medium for the war-dead of past conflicts, who he invites to 'Cry through the trumpet of my fear and rage'.[3] He knows that something which has happened before is happening again, but this does nothing to dull his emotive response, his own 'dreams of artificial hate' and his 'fear and rage' at what might occur.

The poem's excessive length and tendency to slip into high-flown proclamations or imperatives leave it feeling both watered down and inflated: as Jeffrey Wainwright points out, it is 'a bold, torrential poem and cannot be said to succeed as a whole', for all its imaginative accomplishment.[4] But 'The Foreign Gate' has a much terser counterpart in 'Dunbar, 1650', completed later the same spring. This poem was prompted by Keyes being stationed in the Scottish town of the title in June 1942, and evokes the Battle of Dunbar, in which Cromwell's Parliamentarians inflicted a brutal defeat on a loyalist Scottish army. The poem's point of view is selectively omniscient, concentrating on the doomed Scottish army:

> Crossing the little river
> Their pikes jostled and rang.
> The ditches were full of dead
> A blackbird sang.[5]

There is something pathetic about the minuteness of these warriors, their weapons ringing and jostling at the sky as they set about meeting their fate. And the natural world carries on regardless the whole time, as emphasized in that shortened last line of the stanza.

The Scottish poet Hamish Henderson, a committed communist, also saw the war very much through the lens of human history. Henderson served first as an enlisted soldier, but soon joined the Intelligence Corps, partly due to his command of multiple languages. His *Elegies for the Dead in Cyrenaica*, a reflection on civilization and its afflictions, was first published in 1948 but written largely during war service. It is named after a part of the Libyan desert, conquered by successive waves of Greeks, Egyptians, Romans and Arabs, and this history provides a long-view to set against the contemporary experiences the poems record in 'the malevolent bomb-thumped desert', as the 'Second Elegy: Halfaya' puts it (*PSWW* 45).[6] Henderson's greatest influence on the writing associated with the war, however, was as a collector and writer of ballads. The most influential of these was perhaps 'The Ballad of the D-Day Dodgers', a bitterly ironic poem to be sung to the tune of the laconic love song 'Lili Marlene' and published anonymously (as were most of Henderson's ballads). It was a response to the claim made in 1944 by the right-wing erstwhile Nazi sympathizer Lady Nancy Astor that the D-Day landings might be compromised by shirkers on the Mediterranean front:

> Naples and Cassino were taken in our stride,
> We didn't go to fight there – we went there for the ride.
>   Anzio and Sango were just names
>   We only went there to look for dames –
> The artful D Day-Dodgers, way out in Italy.[7]

As the verses accumulate, so too do the ironies. However, at the end the ironic bubble finally bursts and the poem – and the singing Tommies – tell Lady Astor exactly what they think of her and her kind 'talking tommy-rot'. The only 'D-Day dodgers who'll stay in Italy' are those who have, after much 'Heartbreak and toil and suffering', paid the ultimate price and now lie beneath 'scattered crosses'. Few writers of any war have had as much of an impact as Henderson did with this wildly popular poem, but almost none who sang it knew he had written it. It just *existed*, in the way songs, rhymes, jokes and tales so often do.

81

Concerning poetic form as it is more conventionally understood, perhaps the most widely-known poem about the Second World War at the time was by Henry Reed. A native of Birmingham, Reed was conscripted in 1941 and also served in Intelligence – in his case at Bletchley Park, where the Enigma Code was to be broken. Around the time of his conscription he wrote a spirited and oft-quoted pastiche of T. S. Eliot's *Four Quartets* – a 'fifth quartet', if you will – called 'Chard Whitlow'. But his most famous and accomplished poem is 'Naming of Parts', the first section of the five-part sequence 'Lessons of the War', which was published in 1942.[8] A non-commissioned officer is educating new conscripts in the handling of guns, but they do not seem able to keep their minds fully on the job:

> Today we have the naming of parts. Yesterday,
> We had daily cleaning. And tomorrow morning,
> We shall have what to do after firing. But today,
> Today we have naming of parts. Japonica
> Glistens like coral in all of the neighbouring gardens,
> And today we have the naming of parts.

> (*PSWW* 22)

The poem might almost have been called 'Sod's Law': the main problem with the naming of parts seems to be that it is dull, dull, dull, and while they work through it the world outside mocks with its flowers and sunshine and promises of elsewhere. As John Lucas notes, fighting what was widely perceived as being a 'just' war 'makes possible, desirable even, the anti-heroic',[9] and Reed's poem tapped into that spirit. With a balance of wit and warmth, he captures the awkwardness of the neophyte soldiers, the glory of doing anything but naming the parts of a weapon, the tediousness of the instructor, the lassitude that undermines terror (each of the poem's five stanzas follows the same pattern of laconic repetition and gazing out of the window). There is a war to be won, and these new recruits must learn to kill, but all the while they are thinking paradoxically about the temptations of the life that war prevents and destroys, and that still rages on outside.

Strikingly, the lessons they learn seem to concentrate wholly on what happens before and after firing: the act of pulling the trigger on another human being doesn't appear to be on the curriculum. But no training can quite prepare new soldiers for how they are going to react to war, of course. The speaker of John Quinn's 'Men Laughing' recalls that he once laughed the 'bleating, hollow laughter' of the untroubled young man (*PSWW* 42). Now, three years into the war, he listens to the 'Deep, hard laughter' of soldiers, 'Their challenge to blind, stupid fate'. Such laughter is a rebuff of hopelessness. The speaker of F. T. Prince's 'Soldiers Bathing' also relishes the life-affirming joy of soldiers that is sharpened by being a 'challenge to...fate'. The speaker stands apart from 'his soldiers', watching them 'shout and run in the warm air' as 'Their flesh worn by the trade of war revives' (*PSWW* 32).

In Alan Ross's 'Mess Deck', military recruits (this time sailors) take a different kind of refuge from the working lives that have been given to them. Like Causley, Ross served at sea and outside the officer ranks, and here he writes about the unglamorous and un-heroic life of waiting belowdecks for war to happen. In a scene reminiscent of the free time in barracks described by Randall Jarrell in 'Eighth Air Force', sailors in the evening write letters and play ludo 'under naked bulbs', thinking of home and playing games to forget it in equal measure. And, when the time comes,

> We reach for sleep like a gas, randy for oblivion,
> But, laid out on lockers, some get waylaid;
> And lie stiff, running off films in the mind's dark room.
>
> (*PSWW* 35)

'Mess Deck' is a sonnet, a form traditionally used for poems about unrequited love. This poem instead turns to imply a seedy counterpart to unrequited love: masturbating over 'films in the mind'. 'Lie stiff' is a fairly obvious crude pun – as, indeed, is the title.

The waiting for action has come to an abrupt end in Ross's 'Captain's Fur Collar', one of the most startling and even sickening poems to emerge from the Second World War. The subject is a wounded captain, his collar

> Stained and wet as shot rabbit
> And his eye clinging to a thread
> Like spit....
>
> (*PSWW* 103)

The 'spit' simile, and with it the rhyme on 'rabbit', is carried over the second line break – apparently pulled out of its expected place (at the end of the rhyming couplet) much as the eye itself has been. Despite his injuries, however, the captain maintains the highest and most discordant dignity, 'pick[ing] his way from the bridge / With the indifference of a waiter'. But he also hides away to suffer his agony alone – just as the rabbit used in that simile at the start of the poem might have done:

> We found him hours later,
> Bolt upright on the edge
> Of his bunk two decks below,
> Eye dangling like a monocle, face like snow.

This last line is strung out like the eye on its optic nerve; the 'face like snow' belies the agony of the sufferer, despite his calm, and makes it fairly clear he has died. This unfussy man is reminiscent of the officer described in Keith Douglas's 'Aristocrats', one of a 'gentle / obsolescent breed of heroes' who, when found crawling around, says: 'It's most unfair, they've shot my foot off' (*TCP* 117). And the detached and ironic description of a corpse, its eye hanging down like a monocle of all things, is as cool and extrospective as anything by Douglas, and equally visceral: the poem describes and disturbs, its speaker eschewing ostensible pity. We are to make of the facts what we will.

Vernon Scannell is another poet with a direct style. Like Douglas, Scannell served in North Africa and then Normandy. Unlike Douglas, however, he was sent to a military prison in Alexandria, charged with desertion, and eventually discharged with an army record declaring him 'Permanently unfit for military service'.[10] This is something he kept secret for the rest of his life. He didn't write poetry about the war until many years later, either. 'Walking Wounded', completed in 1962, has a directness, objectivity and muscle reminiscent of Douglas, but it is also the poem of a veteran brooding over a now-distant and unchangeable past. The poem begins with post-battle sights, presenting a kind of deathly freeze-frame shot that is repulsive in part because of its absurdity:

> In the ditch at the cross roads the fallen rider lay
> Hugging his dead machine and did not stir
> At crunch of mortar, tantrum of a Bren....

> (*Walking Wounded* 393)

Death is projected from the 'fallen rider' to his equipment, but of course only the man is dead in a literal sense, uncannily and unknowingly hugging what might once have saved him, itself a counterpart to the machine that probably killed him. The poem's main subject is not a dead soldier, though, but the walking wounded of the title 'Straggling the road like convicts loosely chained, / Dragging at ankles exhaustion and despair'. And the speaker, 'remembering after eighteen years', finds that

> In the heart's throat a sour sadness stirs;
> Imagination pauses and returns
> To see them walking still, but multiplied
> In thousands now.

The themes of time and salvation are explored at considerable length in T. S. Eliot's last major work, *Four Quartets*. The final two of the four were written entirely after the outbreak of war, and the last, 'Little Gidding', which is concerned specifically with the element of fire, has too broad a scope to be called a war poem as such but is clearly informed by Eliot's experiences of the London Blitz, during which he worked as an air raid warden. The speaker meets at dawn a 'familiar compound ghost / Both intimate and unidentifiable',[11] and is told that he must be 'restored by that refining fire' (*FQ* 45), before the ghost fades 'on the blowing of the horn' – which might be interpreted as an air raid siren sounding the all-clear. God, the poem ultimately asserts, is key to redemption.

Contemporaneous poets of the First World War wrote during the infancy of modernist experimentation, and those of the Second wrote in the wake of its maturation. But for most poets associated with either conflict, the Eliotian advocacy of impersonality was not very important. Another significant modernist poet, Basil Bunting, completed his three-part poem *The Spoils* in 1951, whilst working for the British Embassy in Tehran.[12] During the Second World War, Bunting had served in British Military Intelligence in Persia, and *The Spoils* draws on that world and circumstance. The poem's final section describes a scene somewhat reminiscent of both the discarded war machinery and animalistic human opportunism presented in Douglas's 'Cairo Jag':

> We marvelled, careful of craters and minefields,
> noting a new-painted recognisance
> on a fragment of fuselage, sand drifting into dumps,
> a tank's turret twisted skyward,
> here and there a lorry unharmed
> out of fuel or the crew scattered.[13]

It is as though that mangled tank is presenting its futile threat to heaven – and with its death and detritus, this is a kind of eerily unpeopled hell on earth. Soon, however, this voyeuristic crew reach 'readymade villages clamped on cornland'. But they too are

> empty, Arabs feeding vines to goats;
> at last orchards aligned, girls hawked by their mothers
> from tent to tent....

Finally we encounter life, then, but it hardly seems a blessing.

As I have noted, though, the sense of apparent futility that hung over much of the 1914–18 war was not in the same sense a condition of 1939–45, and outrage at the necessary cost of war risked seeming utterly inappropriate. The New Zealand-born Australian poet Douglas Stewart's 'Sonnets to an Unknown Soldier', published in 1941, do not contradict this sense of obligation any more than the poems mentioned above, but Stewart is very much aware that the Great War – the 'war to end all wars' – inspired false rhetoric and false hopes in humanity. The title of the sequence makes reference to a Tomb of the Unknown Soldier, a monument to all soldiers killed in war in which one unidentified soldier's body is interred. After the First World War there was a movement to commemorate the war dead with such tombs, and they form part of many war memorials throughout the world. Stewart's sequence of sonnets begins with an angry, dejected poem about how the present generation has let down (or at least exposed the false optimism) of its predecessors who fought that 'war to end all wars'. Stewart implores us to 'break up the monument', remove the regalia, 'Greet him with silence since all the speeches were lies', and hand him fresh khaki and a rifle.[14] The Unknown Soldier 'lives for ever', but only because 'he always comes when they want him. He does the fighting'. The Unknown Soldier, then, is effectively every apparently anonymous soldier sent to kill and be killed – and all of that is happening again. What's more, it always will be happening.

For all the horror of war, though, some of its experiences can be euphoric. John Gillespie Magee, a half-British and British-educated American citizen, enrolled in the Canadian Air Force in October 1940, and trained as a spitfire pilot with the RAF in England. He would be killed in a mid-air collision over Lincolnshire in December the following year, at the age of nineteen. He is remembered now for the sonnet 'High Flight', a commemoration of an experience the service had afforded him, written in the September before his death:

> Oh! I have slipped the surly bonds of Earth
> And danced the skies on laughter-silvered wings...
> And, while with silent, lifting mind I've trod
> The high untrespassed sanctity of space,
> Put out my hand, and touched the face of God.[15]

The poem celebrates the opportunity to confront a frontier. Flying is life-affirming – more than simply exhilarating – for it seems to bring him both literally and metaphorically closer to divinity. For this reason, the poem was put to use in a very different context following the destruction of the Space Shuttle Challenger in 1986, when United States President Ronald Reagan (mis)quoted the first and last lines above in commemoration of the seven astronauts killed that day.[16]

'High Flight' is not so much a poem about war, or training for war, as it is a poem of 'in-spite-of-it-all' euphoria. Preparing to fight was an entirely different phenomenon. Roy Fuller's 'Waiting to be Drafted' is, like several of his war poems, pervaded by an uncanny sense that rather more is happening than is superficially evident. 'It might be any evening of spring', the poem begins, though it ends with a premonition of new recruits' 'bodies' (*PSWW* 23–4). 'Army Reception Centre', by the Canadian poet Raymond Souster, describes being called up for what seemed a 'far-off war' – geographically but perhaps also emotionally – and seeing the returning wounded 'sat around in the corridors / with arms or legs missing / waiting for discharge' (*PSWW* 46). It is a stark and sudden reminder of where he will eventually be sent, half a world and a whole war away from Fredericton, New Brunswick, where the poem is set. Comparably, in Howard Nemerov's short 'Grand Central, With Soldiers, In Early Morning', new servicemen wait to board a train in New York and begin their journey to war: they 'go in stealth and leave no trace / In early morning before business starts' (*PSWW* 30). When the working day dawns in America's greatest city, the soldiers will have vanished. For them to be noticed departing, with no promise of return, might damage civilian morale: it is better for home morale if most of the public are not reminded about the war and what it can mean any more than is absolutely necessary.

But this highlights a contrast between the home fronts in North America and in Britain, where war was brought to civilians in the form of sustained bombing raids. The last stanza of W. H. Auden's 'September 1, 1939', surely the most famous poem about the beginning of any war, begins by evoking 'Our world in stupor', lying 'Defenceless under the night' (*PSWW* 11). Two years after the Luftwaffe's aerial bombardment of 'defenceless' Guernica in the Spanish Civil War, the threat of attack from the sky was for many to remain very real – though not in America, where the English poet had recently moved and where the poem is set, 'in one of the dives / On Fifty-Second Street' in Manhattan. By the time the USA joined the war at the end of 1941,[17] over 40,000 people in Britain had been killed by the Luftwaffe in bombing raids: in Britain, and throughout much of Europe and other parts of the world, the Second World War was a civilian's war as well as a soldier's one. This is, inevitably, reflected in much of the poetry from the time. Roy Fuller's 'London Air-Raid, 1940' notes, with more feeling than originality, that 'Tonight humanity is trapped in evil'.[18] Edith Sitwell's 'Still Falls the Rain', subtitled 'The Raids, 1940. Night and Dawn', begins with a meditation on the similarity between this 'Rain' and the equally 'Blind' 'nineteen hundred and forty nails' – one for each year – 'Upon the cross' (*PSWW* 63). Our capacity to cause suffering is perennial. Sitwell's is a laborious poem, which cannot be said about E. J. Scovell's four-line 'Days Drawing In', the main subject of which is an infant girl. Scovell takes a personal rather than a catholic view, but her poem ends with short-lived relief at a bombing raid being over for one night: 'Sweet the grey morning and the raiders gone' (*PSWW* 59). Scovell lived in Oxford, a city targeted less by the Luftwaffe than most in Britain (though the threat was always present), but she had grown up in a suburb of Sheffield, one of the country's most comprehensively bombed cities. The streets she had known as a child were being turned to rubble.

The Welsh poet R. S. Thomas was further from harm's way. Thomas, a clergyman, was exempt from military service, and though he helped to organize the distribution of evacuees in his parish, living in rural Wales kept him relatively far from the machinations of war. Luftwaffe bombing raids on nearby Merseyside ensured they could not be forgotten, however. In his book-length autobiographical poem *The Echoes Return Slow*, published in 1988 when he was an old man, he remembers that 'Skies were red where no / sun had ever risen', teaching him 'the instinctive fear / of the animal that finds / the foliage about its den / disarranged'.[19] The much earlier 'Homo Sapiens 1941', written in that year of the war, was presumably influenced by the same experience of hearing and seeing German bombers flying overhead. Its title, however, takes in the whole of the human race at that particular point in history:

> Murmuration of engines in the cold caves of air,
> And, daring the starlight above the stiff sea of cloud,
> Deadly as a falcon brooding over its prey
> In a tower of spirit-dazzling and splendid light,
> Pedestrian man holds grimly on his way.[20]

The falcon-airman (the absence of a comma after 'prey' momentarily leaves open both possibilities, reinforcing the congruence between predator-bird and predator-aircraft) appears as if suspended upon the 'tower' of a searchlight. He is simultaneously isolated in 'cold caves of air' and also the focus of attention, a 'pedestrian' and anything but pedestrian – in both senses of that word. The tone and subject call to mind Yeats's 'An Irish Airman Foresees His Death', written during the First World War: 'A lonely impulse of delight / Drove to this tumult in the clouds. / I balanced all....'[21] But the shift to third person gives Thomas's poem a greater sense of objectivity, and the absence of a national or local identity makes the subject all the more ecumenical: Yeats's airman identifies with 'Kiltartan's poor' in an Ireland still under British rule, whereas Thomas's airman is Everyairman. Moreover, Yeats's airman knows he is going to die, whereas Thomas's, a year into Blitzkrieg, seems invincible. But at its end, the poem refers to the airman's 'delicate wings' before telling us he is mantled 'like a god': he is *not* a god, and we are invited to remember the hubris of Icarus, and *his* 'delicate wings'. The 'murmuration' overhead terrorizes, but is also a symbol of human delusions of grandeur.

Perhaps the most shocking, tender and original poem about the bombing of Britain is 'A Refusal to Mourn the Death, by Fire, of a Child in London' by another Welshman, Dylan Thomas. The child subject of the poem would typically be regarded as a tragic victim, an innocent who cannot possibly bear any responsibility for the world of carnage into which she has been born and out of which she has been so violently removed. The poem focuses instead on endless cycles of tumult, accretion, and coming-into-being, assisted by the compression and repetition of its ABCABC rhyme scheme:

> Never until the mankind making
> Bird beast and flower
> Fathering and all humbling darkness
> Tells with silence the last light breaking
> And the still hour
> Is come of the sea tumbling in harness....

(PSWW 70)

The first three of the poem's four six-line stanzas comprise two sentences and, apart from the two full-stops, are unpunctuated. Always we are kept pushing on, striving to make sense of the sentences across the enjambments, until the brakes come on as we arrive at the grave and memorable climax, where attention turns squarely to the girl lying 'Deep with the first dead' by the 'unmourning water' of the Thames. The last line of the poem, also by far its shortest sentence, has the weight of the maxim: 'After the first death there is no other.'

What about the view of bombing from those in the air, above the targets? 'Massive Retaliation', by the American poet John Ciardi, concerns the bombing of Japan after the US capture (from the Japanese) of the Pacific island of Saipan in 1944. The poem has an intriguing title, suggesting a less than noble, even un-Christian, justification for the attack. Ciardi recalls 'watching the shore towns blow / like spouts below us', a 'searchlight from the world' shining up at them, and looking down at 'one more thing to set fire to' (*PSWW* 91). This isn't so much a refusal to mourn death as a failure fully to acknowledge it. As twenty-first century opponents of military drones point out, it is relatively easy to cause destruction in 'the world' when you feel divorced from it yourself. Ciardi's airman has become the startling apotheosis of R. S. Thomas's hubristic man mantled 'like a god'.

After the Nazi surrender, in May 1945, the war against Japan continued until the Japanese surrender on 15 August. This occurred just days after the first (and still only) atomic bombings in any war, carried out by the US Air Force on the cities of Hiroshima on 6 August and Nagasaki three days later. Debate still rages over whether the bombings significantly shortened the war or not, and the Russians were poised on the ground to force the surrender of the hugely depleted Japanese military. At any rate, for many thousands in and around Hiroshima and Nagasaki it was devastating: up to 125,000 people were killed in both cities on the days of the bombings, roughly the same number succumbed to injury or radiation poisoning in the following four months, and many thousands more *hibakusha*, or 'explosion-affected persons', died later still from their exposure. Both cities were all but flattened. Marc Kaminsky's 'Carrying My Brother' follows testimony from *Death in Life: Survivors of Hiroshima*, edited by Robert Jay Lifton (New York: Random House, 1968). The poem begins:

> I am still on the road to the doctor's house
> carrying my brother
> in my arms....[22]

(PSWW 192)

The context implies that the brother is suffering the acute effects of radiation. However, he appears initially to have recovered somewhat: 'he is going to survive', the speaker thinks to himself. Then the brother dies in his arms, and the speaker is left facing the prospect that the silent killer might yet get him too: 'I am always on the road to the doctor', the poem ends, with a foreboding echo of the opening line. His own *apparent* health is no guarantee of it: he also is one of the *hibakusha*.

No destruction in the Second World War, however, came close to matching the Holocaust for sheer scale and brutality.

The systematic murder of six million Jews, gypsies, disabled people, homosexuals and others deemed undeserving of life by the Nazis only became widely and fully known about after the Nazi defeat. Despite Theodor Adorno's dictum from 1949 – often repeated out of context and as though it has ultimate authority – that 'To write poetry after Auschwitz is barbaric', many poets have naturally tried to find a way to write about the final journeys, the bitter separations, the concentration camps, the torture, the gas chambers.

One such poet is Lily Brett, who was born in 1946 in one of the newly established displaced persons camps in Germany. Her parents had spent much of the war confined to the squalor of the ghetto in Łódź, Poland, before being transferred to Auschwitz. There they were separated, only finding one another several months after the end of the war in Europe. As she puts it in 'People Weeping', 'I was born / in the middle / of a provisional government' among 'angry / restless guests / in Germany' (*PSWW* 239–40). Brett writes in a very direct fashion about the horrors experienced by so many of her parents' generation in Nazi-occupied Europe: 'in Auschwitz / she fed her friend snow / when she was burning with typhoid', she writes in 'My Mother's Friend' (*PSWW* 241). Charles Reznikoff's *Holocaust* (1975) is similarly unadorned. Reznikoff was a prominent poet of the Objectivist movement, a group of poets concerned with, in Louis Zukofsky's phrase, 'Sincerity and Objectification' – something close in its way to the 'extrospective' style Keith Douglas aimed for:

> In the gas chambers
> the police wedged the people closely together
> until men and women were standing on the feet of each other
> and the doors were closed.
> But the engine to furnish the gas
> could not start.

> (*PSWW* 172)

The unequal lines give the poem a jittery, disorienting feel. After a while, the machinery springs to life and soon enough the bodies can be raided for scrap like cars at a breaker's yard:

> Two dozen workers were busy
> opening the mouths of the dead with iron hooks
> and with chisels taking out teeth with golden caps....

Little could be more emotive than the discrepancy between the objective tone and what is being described – which in turn reminds us that, to the perpetrators of such acts, no such discrepancy existed.

One of the finest poets to write about the Holocaust in English was Anthony Hecht. Hecht was born in New York in 1923 to German-Jewish parents, and in 1944 was sent with the US Army to Czechoslovakia and to his parents' original homeland. On April 1945, he took part in the liberation of Flossenbürg, an annex of the more famous Buchenwald camp, and thereafter he was involved in interviewing survivors to supply evidence for the Flossenbürg war crimes trial. Throughout his short time as a soldier, Hecht had, by his own admission, experienced 'a lot of terrible things', but nothing to match the horrors of Flossenbürg, and the experience was almost too much for him: 'Prisoners were dying at the rate of 500 a day...from typhus. The place, the suffering, the prisoners' accounts were beyond comprehension. For years after I would wake shrieking.'[23]

Some of this would appear to make its way into 'More Light! More Light!', perhaps the single most affecting short poem about the Holocaust. The title allegedly comprises the opaque final words of Goethe; in the context of Hecht's poem, these words imply both a desire to shed metaphorical light and to soak it up. The poem evokes two ideological and protracted executions at different points in European history. The first of these is a burning at the stake in what appears to be Renaissance England. Hecht provides few contextual details beyond 'the Tower' (of London?), but the narrative brings to mind such episodes as the burning of Protestant martyrs in the sixteenth century, during the reign of Queen Mary. The second execution is the burial alive and shooting of two Jews and a Pole in a Nazi concentration camp.

Though both of the poem's narratives are horrific, the differences between them are quite marked. The earlier execution has been planned: the victim knew he was to be executed, and when, and before his execution composed 'moving verses' and 'implore[d] my God to witness that I have made no crime'.[24] As he burned to death, 'such as were by made prayers in the name of Christ'. His executioners also appear to have attempted some level of mercy by adding gunpowder to the pyre, though it has failed to ignite and the death 'was horrible': 'His legs were blistered sticks on which the black sap / Bubbled and burst as he howled for the Kindly Light.' The 'Kindly Light' here is the erstwhile darkness of death: the combined prayers of executed and executioner have done nothing to make his journey to the other side anything less than agonizing and sickening.

In the later scene, we move not only from Renaissance England to twentieth-century Germany, but also from the past tense to the immediacy of a present-tense narrative. The setting is a wood 'beyond the hill' from Goethe's shrine at Weimar, suggesting that the poem is set at Buchenwald. A German officer orders a Pole to bury two Jews alive. He refuses, so the Jews are instead ordered to bury the Pole – then, when he is up to his 'quivering chin', to dig him out again. The Pole is ordered once more to bury the Jews, does so, and is then shot in the stomach, dying a protracted death 'three hours' later. The poem ends with a grotesque image of his body being covered with the ashes of the cremated: 'Ghosts from the ovens, sifting through crisp air', which 'settled upon his eyes in a black soot'.

The Jews are never individualized in the poem, and the German is defined metonymically only by his Luger pistol. Though interaction between four people is described in these final five stanzas, the main focus is on the Pole, and we are therefore encouraged in particular to compare and contrast his slow death to that of the man burned at the stake in the first three stanzas. The tone of the poem is level, devoid of ostensible outrage, in a manner reminiscent of Reznikoff, but in Hecht's poem a moral judgement is nonetheless very evident: the second death, and execution, is fundamentally more horrific and degrading than the first, and not only because more people die. By refusing orders, the Pole initially clings to the 'light' of human empathy and heroism, something that has already been vanquished for the two Jews whose souls have 'drained away' because of 'Much casual death'. But the Pole's ordeal soon breaks him too, and following his near-burial and exhumation, there is 'no light, no light in the blue Polish eye' either. The *Untermenschen* are all dehumanized – broken before they are forced to kill (or believe they are killing) and then killed in turn.

Moreover, their deaths are compared, directly and indirectly, to that of the victim in the opening stanzas. As the Pole dies, 'No prayers or incense' fill the air, and the two suffocating Jews are buried both literally and figuratively, being all but forgotten about in the last lines of the poem. Their deaths were perhaps the most 'horrible' and protracted of all, but unlike the other deaths theirs are overlooked entirely, in what is a daring act of pointed complicity with the Nazi perspective. The victim of the first three stanzas was 'Permitted at least his pitiful dignity' and died amid Christian prayers; the Pole and the Jews are destroyed internally before being destroyed externally, and die without ceremony.

For many survivors, on all fronts, the effects of the Second World War continued after the surrender documents had been signed and peace had resumed. As New Zealander James K. Baxter puts it in the sonnet 'Returned Soldier', 'The boy who volunteered at seventeen / At twenty-three is heavy on the booze': the six years have left him ruined, desperate for release (*PSWW* 236). But beneath the unforgettable experiences of war, and uncovered only in dreams, is a suddenly-truncated youth of 'leaves and flowers / Remembered girls'. Non-combatants continued also to feel the aftershocks of conflict. Ruth Pitter's 'Victory Bonfire', a poem of the Home Front in England, describes a firework display and pyre celebrating victory – evidently staged a month after those final events in Japan, for it is a 'sweet September' evening. This celebration calls to mind Guy Fawkes Night, celebrated throughout much of Britain each November, during which effigies of the Gunpowder Plot ringleader are burned on bonfires and fireworks are set off. But on this occasion the crowd has a contemporary villain: 'high-climbing boys had planted an image of Hitler / On the lonely summit' (*PSWW* 221). For six years, blackouts had rendered such bonfires and firework displays impossible in Britain, and now that people were able to resume this common form of celebration it had been tainted, 'For a rocket can only be a V2, / A firecracker a thermite bomb'. Thermite was the key active ingredient in most incendiary bombs in the war, and the German V-2 rockets – the world's first long-range ballistic missiles, that exploded without any possibility for air-raid warnings – were first used by the Germans in the last year of the war and were specifically targeted at London. The crowd are 'not quite sure how they like' these more benign rockets and controlled fires that now evoke so much experienced and witnessed tragedy and horror. But nor are they prepared to allow their traditional form of celebration to be undermined by what they have endured. As was the case for so many of the poets who survived the war, they have been changed by it. But they will never be so naïve as to think they have survived a war to end all wars. And they certainly hadn't.

Notes

CHAPTER 1. INTRODUCTION: WHERE WERE THE WAR POETS?

1. This was turned into an essay, 'The Poets of World War Two', the following year. See Robert Graves, *The Common Asphodel* (Hamish Hamilton, 1949).
2. Rupert Brooke, *Collected Poems* (Oleander, 2010), 135.
3. Isaac Rosenberg (1890–1918) was a poet of the First World War.
4. Michael Foss, 'Introduction', in *Poetry of the World Wars*, ed. Michael Foss (Michael O'Mara Books, 1990), 107–9 at 108.
5. This remained popular for much of the twentieth century, being included in such places as *The Oxford Book of Twentieth Century English Verse*, ed. Philip Larkin (Oxford University Press, 1973), 353. Originally published in Cecil Day-Lewis, *Word Over All* (Cape, 1943).
6. In *The Poetry of War: 1939–45*, ed. Ian Hamilton (New English Library, 1972), 169.
7. Many fine poets of other languages are included in translation in *Poetry of the Second World War*, ed. Douglas Graham (Pimlico, 1998).

CHAPTER 2. KEITH DOUGLAS

1. Quoted in William Scammell, *Keith Douglas: A Study* (Faber, 1988), 207.
2. Desmond Graham, *Keith Douglas 1920–1944* (Oxford University Press, 1974), 109.
3. Ted Hughes, 'Introduction', in Keith Douglas, *The Complete Poems* (3rd edn.), ed. Desmond Graham (Faber, 1998), xxii.
4. Blunden passed this to T. S. Eliot, the editor at Faber and Faber, who praised Douglas's talent but declined to offer publication.
5. Rupert Brooke, *Collected Poems* (Oleander, 2010), 139.

6. Wilfred Owen, *The Poems of Wilfred Owen* (Wordsworth, 1994), 99.
7. Here Douglas unwittingly echoes Alun Lewis's 'After Dunkirk', discussed in the next chapter.
8. Charles Baudelaire, *Poems*, ed. and trans. Carol Clark (Penguin, 1995), 6.
9. Letter to J. C. Hall, 10 August 1943, reprinted in *The Complete Poems*, 135.
10. John 20.23, King James Version.
11. Keith Douglas, *Alamein to Zem Zem*, ed. Desmond Graham (Oxford University Press, 1979), 29.
12. It should be remembered, however, that the instruction for the reader to 'look', when given in a poem, cannot hope to be literal.
13. Quoted in Scammell, 208.
14. Wilfred Owen, *The Poems of Wilfred Owen* (Wordsworth, 1994), 95.
15. Robert Graves, *The Complete Poems* (Penguin, 2003), 27.
16. Isaac Rosenberg (1890–1918), poet of the First World War.

CHAPTER 3. ALUN LEWIS

1. Of course, some poets who write memorably of war and then, like Causley, live on for many years, such as Edmund Blunden and Siegfried Sassoon, *do* continue to be known almost entirely as 'war poets'.
2. Ian Hamilton, *Against Oblivion: Some Lives of the Twentieth-Century Poets* (Penguin, 2003), 233.
3. Quoted in John Pikoulis, *Alun Lewis: A Life* (Seren, 1991), 72.
4. Alun Lewis, *Letters to My Wife*, ed. Gweno Lewis (Seren, 1989), 101.
5. Pikoulis, 82.
6. Edward Thomas, *Selected Poems of Edward Thomas*, ed. R. S. Thomas (Faber, 1964), 42.
7. Quoted in Pikoulis, 95–6.
8. 'Aubade', Philip Larkin, *Collected Poems*, ed. Anthony Thwaite (Faber, 1988), 209.
9. R. S. Thomas, *Collected Poems: 1945–1990* (Phoenix, 1993), 4. Thomas's first book was not published until after Lewis's death, though some of his poems (including the one quoted here, 'A Peasant') had appeared in periodicals throughout the war.
10. See 'If War Comes – Will I Fight?', in *Alun Lewis: A Miscellany of His Writings*, ed. John Pikoulis (Seren, 1982), 81–5.
11. Quoted in Pikoulis, 186.
12. Rainer Maria Rilke, *Letters to a Young Poet*, trans. Stephen Mitchell (Vintage, 1986), 14.

CHAPTER 4. RANDALL JARRELL

1. David Perkins, *A History of Modern Poetry: Modernism and After* (Harvard University Press, 1987), 393.
2. Robert Lowell, 'Randall Jarrell, 1914–1965', in *New York Review of Books* (25 November 1965).
3. John Lucas, *Second World War Poetry in English* (Greenwich Exchange, 2013), 85.
4. These poems by Keith Douglas are discussed in the relevant chapter of this study.
5. 'Then said Pilate to the chief priests and to the people, I find no fault in this man', Luke 23.4, King James Version. Jarrell adds the word 'just', itself a pun for 'only'.
6. This poem by Charles Causley is discussed in the relevant chapter of this study.
7. Richard Fein, 'Randall Jarrell's World of War', in Suzanne Ferguson, (ed.), *Critical Essays on Randall Jarrell* (Hall, 1983), 157.
8. Jarrell's notes to some of the poems are there to elucidate, and as the poet puts it in his introduction to his *Selected Poems*, 'they are here for the reader only if he wants them' (reprinted in Jarrell, *CP*, 4). But they also channel readers into a 'correct' reading of the poem that can occasionally be restrictive.
9. Stephen Burt, *Randall Jarrell and His Age* (Columbia University Press, 2002), 134–5.

CHAPTER 5. CHARLES CAUSLEY

1. Charles Causley, 'A Kitchen in the Morning', *Causley at 70*, ed. Harry Chambers (Peterloo, 1987), 97.
2. Causley remembers discovering these 'war poets' at an early age: 'In my teens, on a first visit to London, I bought for one-and-six in the Charing Cross Road, a red-covered copy of *The War Poems of Siegfried Sassoon*. It was my first clear view of my father's world of 1914–18, and I went on to read Graves, Blunden, Owen.' 'A Kitchen in the Morning', 104.
3. Raymond Gardner, 'Voice from the Edge', interview with Charles Causley, *The Guardian*, 27 August 1975, 8.
4. Charles Causley, *Secret Destinations*, BBC Radio 3 (25 October 1985). Transcript in the Charles Causley Archive, University of Exeter, at LIT/1/58.
5. In John Mole, 'Charles Causley: Popular Poet with a Primal Insight', *The Independent*, 6 November 2003, 22.

6. Charles Causley, 'Charles Causley', *The Poetry of War: 1939–1945*, ed. Ian Hamilton (New English Library, 1972), 158.
7. Charles Causley, 'Foreword: A Glass of Salt Water', *Hands to Dance and Skylark* (Robson Books, 1979), 10.
8. Rudyard Kipling, *Barrack-Room Ballads*, is a collection of martial poems and songs published in two instalments, in 1892 and 1896.
9. This is undated. Causley Archive, Exeter, at LIT/4/6.
10. Barea would die in 1957, while still in exile in England. During the Second World War his voice would have been familiar to Causley and many other allied men and women in the services, as he worked for the BBC World Service.
11. T. S. Eliot, 'The Waste Land' (1922), in *The Waste Land and Other Poems* (Faber, 1999), 30.
12. Charles Causley, *Survivor's Leave* (Hand and Flower, 1953), 31.
13. Linda M. Shires, *British Poetry of the Second World War* (Macmillan 1985), 69.
14. Louis MacNeice, *Selected Poems*, ed. W. H. Auden (Faber, 1964), 29.
15. Susan Hill, 'Joking Apart', *The Guardian* (15 November 2003), 37.
16. Rupert Brooke, *Collected Poems* (Oleander, 2010), 139.

CHAPTER 6. LOUIS SIMPSON

1. See William Shakespeare, *Hamlet*, V, i.
2. John Lucas, *Second World War Poetry in English* (London: Greenwich Exchange, 2013), 175.
3. The Purple Heart is a US military honour, awarded to those wounded or killed on active service.
4. Louis Simpson and Laurence R. Smith, 'A Conversation with Louis Simpson', in *Chicago Review* 27.1 (1975), 99–109, at 102.
5. Lucas, 179.
6. The cathedral in that city, Notre-Dame de Reims, does not in fact have a spire, in the true sense: it is possible Simpson had a different church in mind. It does, however, have a sizeable pinnacle above the chevet, at the east end of the building.
7. Siegfried Sassoon, *The War Poems of Siegfried Sassoon* (Dodo, 2007), 47.
8. Both of the Keith Douglas poems mentioned here are discussed earlier in this study, in the chapter on Douglas. In 1957, Douglas's poetry was still yet to become widely known; whether or not Simpson had read it when he was working on 'The Runner', he had experienced the cold winter of 1944–5: unlike the young Douglas, he wrote about freezing corpses as one who had probably seen them.

9. Grevel Lindop, 'On Louis Simpson's *Selected*', in *New Walk* 1 (2010), 36–9, at 38.

CHAPTER 7. NAMING OF PARTS: SOME OTHER POETS OF THE SECOND WORLD WAR

1. John Donne, *The Complete Poems* (Penguin, 1996), 313.
2. Drummond Allison, *The Collected Poems of Drummond Allison*, ed. Stephen Benson (Anthony Rowe, 1994).
3. Sidney Keyes, *Collected Poems* (Carcanet, 2002), 58.
4. Jeffrey Wainwright, 'Introduction', in Sidney Keyes, *Collected Poems*, xi.
5. Keyes, 74.
6. Where possible, references for poems in this chapter refer to *Poetry of the Second World War: An International Anthology*, ed. Desmond Graham (Pimlico, 1998).
7. Hamish Henderson, *Collected Poems and Songs* (Curly Snake, 2000).
8. In *New Statesman and Nation* 24, no. 598 (8 August 1942), 92. Reed's only collection of poems, *A Map of Verona*, was published in 1946.
9. John Lucas, *Second World War Poetry in English* (Greenwich Exchange, 2013), 57.
10. In James Andrew Taylor, *Walking Wounded: The Life and Poetry of Vernon Scannell* (Oxford University Press, 2013), 149.
11. T. S. Eliot, *Four Quartets* (Faber, 1959), 44.
12. The poem wasn't published until 1965.
13. Basil Bunting, *Complete Poems* (Bloodaxe, 2000), 56.
14. Douglas Stewart, *Selected Poems* (Angus and Robertson, 1973).
15. *The Nation's Favourite Poems* (BBC, 1996), 72.
16. Ronald W. Reagan, 'Explosion of the Space Shuttle Challenger: Address to the Nation, 28 January 1986', NASA History Office (2004) <http://history.nasa.gov/reagan12886.html> [accessed 17 December 2013] para. 11 of 12.
17. The Japanese effectively declared war on the USA by attacking the naval base at Pearl Harbor, Hawaii, on 7 December 1941; on 11 December Germany, in solidarity, also declared itself at war with the US, and the other Axis powers followed suit. The US was suddenly fully embroiled in the war.
18. Roy Fuller, *The Individual and His Times: A Selection of the Poetry of Roy Fuller*, ed. V. J. Lee (Athlone, 1982), 49.
19. R. S. Thomas, *Collected Later Poems* (Bloodaxe, 2004), 20.
20. R. S. Thomas, *The Stones of the Field* (Druid, 1946), 12.
21. W. B. Yeats, *The Collected Poems* (Wordsworth Editions, 2000), 111.

22. Being written many years after the end of the war, this poem is among those falling into the category of poetry about the Second World War rather than of it. There is no contemporaneous poetry written in English, so far as I am aware, about these bombings from a civilian, Japanese perspective.

23. Anthony Hecht, *Anthony Hecht in Conversation*, ed. Philip Hoy (London: Between the Lines, 2001).

24. Anthony Hecht, *Selected Poems* (Alfred A. Knopf, 2011), 62.

Select Bibliography

Alldritt, Keith, *Modernism in the Second World War: The Later Poetry of Ezra Pound, T. S. Eliot, Basil Bunting, and Hugh MacDiarmid* (Peter Lang, 1989). Explores the work of these modernist poets – not usually considered in discussions of war poetry – in relation to the Second World War.

Drummond, Allison, *The Collected Poems of Drummond Allison*, ed. Stephen Benson (Anthony Rowe, 1994). The most up-to-date collection of Allison's poetry. Informative introduction.

Bolton, Jonathan, *Personal Landscapes: British Poets in Egypt during the Second World War* (Palgrave Macmillan, 1997). Takes its title from a 1940s periodical publishing British poets in Egypt (including Keith Douglas). Makes a convincing case for the importance of the periodical and the poetry it published.

Burt, Stephen, *Randall Jarrell and His Age* (Columbia University Press, 2002). An engaging and provocative study considering Jarrell in his critical and cultural contexts.

Causley, Charles, *Collected Poems: 1951–2000* (Picador, 2000). The most comprehensive volume of the poet's work.

——, *Hands to Dance and Skylark* (Robson Books, 1979). Short stories, largely about experiences in the navy.

Chambers, Harry (ed.), *Causley at 70* (Peterloo, 1987). A *festschrift*, full of perspectives on Causley's work and poems responding to Causley, and also containing two biographical essays by Causley about his youth.

Davies, Ross, *Drummond Allison: Come, Let Us Pity Death* (Cecil Woolf, 2009). One of the most recent biographies of a poet of the Second World War, with close readings and contextual information.

Douglas, Keith, *Alamein to Zem Zem*, ed. John Waller, G. S. Fraser and J. C. Hall (Faber, 1966). Douglas's first-hand account of the campaign, recounting several experiences that also appear to be behind some of the poems.

——, *Complete Poems*, ed. Desmond Graham (Faber, 2011). The most comprehensive collection of Douglas's poetry, with thorough notes, an introduction by Ted Hughes, and two statements on poetry by Douglas.

————, *A Prose Miscellany*, ed. Desmond Graham (Carcanet, 1985). A varied selection of Douglas's prose, containing letters, short stories about the war, an essay on poetry and the war, and other writings.

————, *The Letters*, ed. Desmond Graham (Carcanet, 2000). Includes many written during the war. Also includes short stories and his essay on poetry in the Second World War.

Ferguson, Suzanne (ed.), *Critical Essays on Randall Jarrell* (Hall, 1983). Still a fine introduction to critical perspectives on Jarrell.

Foss, Michael (ed.), *Poetry of the World Wars* (Michael O'Mara, 1990). An attractive anthology providing an overview of the poems from both wars. No contents page, however, which makes poems hard to locate.

Gardner, Brian (ed.), *The Terrible Rain: The War Poets 1939–1945* (Methuen, 1966). A fairly thorough anthology of poetry about and from the war, arranged around a history of the conflict.

Graham, Desmond, *Keith Douglas 1920–1944: A Biography* (Oxford University Press, 1974).

Graham, Desmond (ed.), *Poetry of the Second World War: An International Anthology* (Pimlico, 1998). Sensitively brings together English-language poetry with poetry in translation from all over the world, and thus provides a more comprehensive overview than any other anthology of poetry from the Second World War.

Green, Laurence. *All Cornwall Thunders at My Door: A Biography of Charles Causley* (Cornovia, 2013). The first book-length biography of Causley.

Hamilton, Ian (ed.), *The Poetry of War: 1939–45* (New English Library, 1972). An anthology with a specific focus on British poets (and some Americans) who served in the military between 1939 and 1945.

Hecht, Anthony, *Anthony Hecht in Conversation*, ed. Philip Hoy (Between the Lines, 2001). A long interview, including discussion of Hecht's experiences of the war.

————, *Selected Poems* (Alfred A. Knopf, 2011). Includes his most important poems about wartime.

Jarrell, Randall, *The Complete Poems* (Noonday, 1969).

————, *The Letters of Randall Jarrell*, ed. Mary Jarrell (Houghton Mifflin, 1985). Includes letters about Jarrell's wartime experiences.

————, *No Other Book: Selected Essays*, ed. Brad Leithauser (Perennial, 2000). A good selection of Jarrell's highly engaging and spirited critical prose.

Kendall, Tim, *Modern English War Poetry* (Oxford University Press, 2006). An astute and passionate assessment of English war poetry throughout and beyond the twentieth century – the finest book of its kind. Useful also for putting the poetry of the Second World War in its broader literary and historical contexts.

Keyes, Sidney, *Collected Poems*, ed. Michael Meyer (Carcanet, 2002). Includes an appendix of memoirs and useful notes on the poems.

Lewis, Alun, *Collected Poems of Alun Lewis*, ed. Cary Archard (Seren, 1994).

———, *Letters to My Wife*, ed. Gweno Lewis (Seren, 1989). Letters mainly written during military service, and providing a context for some of the poems.

———, *Alun Lewis: A Miscellany of His Writings*, ed. John Pikoulis (Seren, 1982). An intriguing selection of the poet's other writings.

Lucas, John, *Second World War Poetry in English* (Greenwich Exchange, 2013). Argues that the common assumptions about the inferiority of poetry from the Second World War should be challenged. An idiosyncratic, opinionated and highly readable survey.

Pikoulis, John, *Alun Lewis: A Life* (Seren, 1991). A thorough biography, full of anecdotes and archival insights.

Rawlinson, Mark, *British Writing of the Second World War* (Clarendon, 2000). A detailed critical and historical survey of British literary culture during the war. Extensive bibliography.

Scammell, William, *Keith Douglas: A Study* (Faber, 1988). Comprehensive and engaging, with a focus on the prose as well as the poems, and also discussing Douglas's critical reception in the 40 years after his death.

Scannell, Vernon, *Not Without Glory: Poets of the Second World War* (Woburn, 1976). A still-useful critical study of (mainly British) poets of the Second World War, making a strong case that the poetry of that conflict is wrongly neglected.

Serdiville, Rosie and John Sadler, *Ode to Bully Beef: WWII Poetry They Didn't Let You Read* (History Press, 2014). Part critical survey, part anthology, this is an engaging, contextualized collection of songs and rhymes, many of which are charming doggerel, shared by Anglophone servicemen and -women in the Second World War.

Shires, Linda M., *British Poetry of the Second World War* (Macmillan 1985). Often insightful – though also Anglocentric.

Simpson, Louis, *The Owner of the House: New Collected Poems 1940–2001* (BOA Editions, 2003). The most comprehensive single volume of Simpson's poetry.

———, *Voices in the Distance: Selected Poems 1940–2009* (Bloodaxe, 2010). Includes poems from Simpson's last collection, *Struggling Times* (2009), alongside selections of his earlier work. Unfortunately rather thin in its representation of Simpson's first three collections.

Taylor, James Andrew, *Walking Wounded: The Life and Poetry of Vernon*

Scannell (Oxford University Press, 2013). A thorough biography with some fine close readings of Scannell's most significant war poems. Also includes some of Scannell's war poems in the appendix, including 'Walking Wounded'.

Index